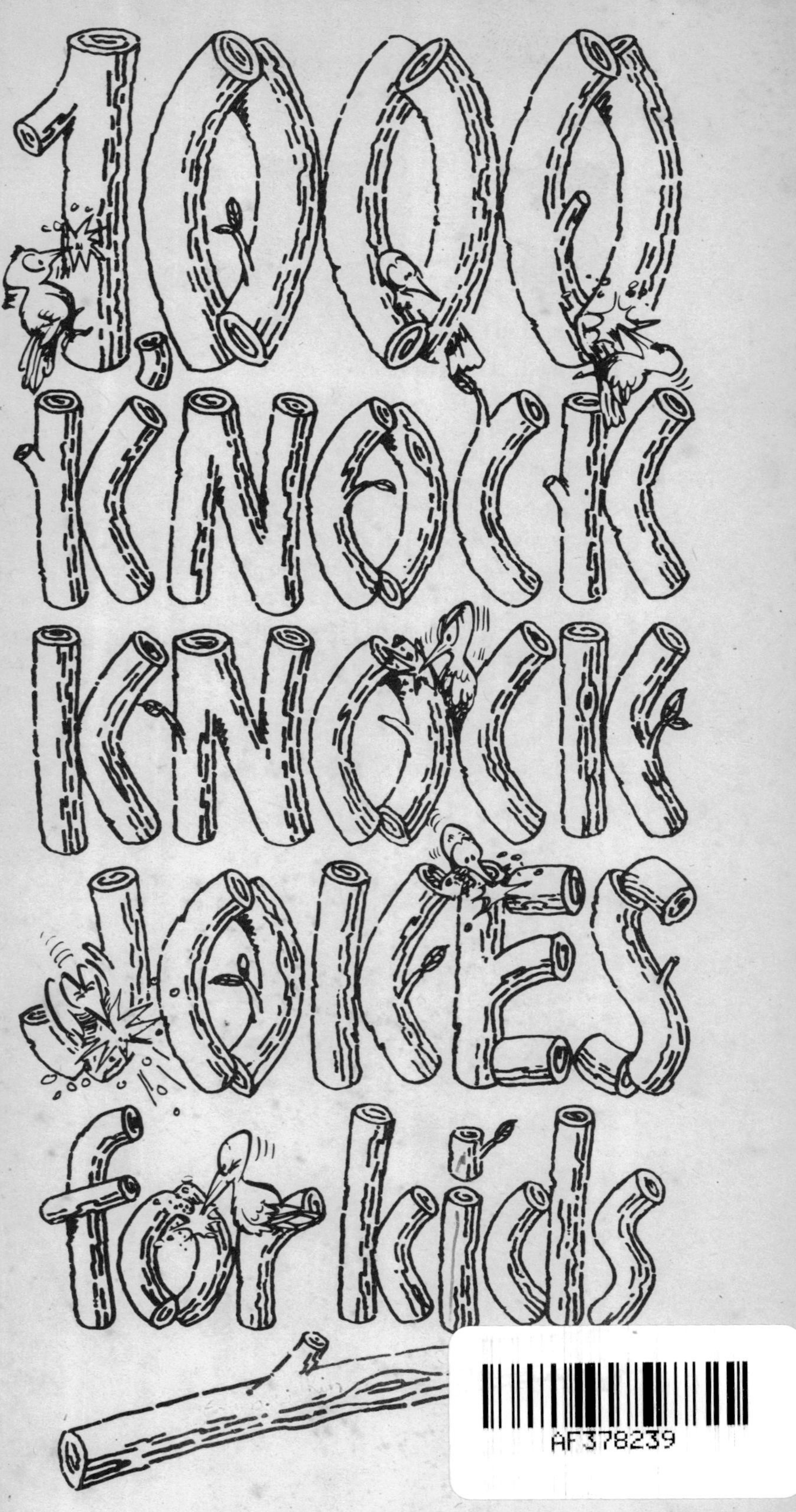

Illustrations by Heather Munro

WARD LOCK LIMITED · LONDON

First published in Great Britain in 1985
by Ward Lock Limited, 8 Clifford Street,
London W1X 1RB.

Reprinted 1987

Text set in Times
by Spire Print Services Ltd, Salisbury, England.

Printed and bound in Finland

British Library Cataloguing in Publication Data

1000 knock-knock jokes.
  1. Wit and humor, Juvenile   2. English
  wit and humor
  828'.91402'0809282   PZ8.7

ISBN 0-7063-6348-5

Contents

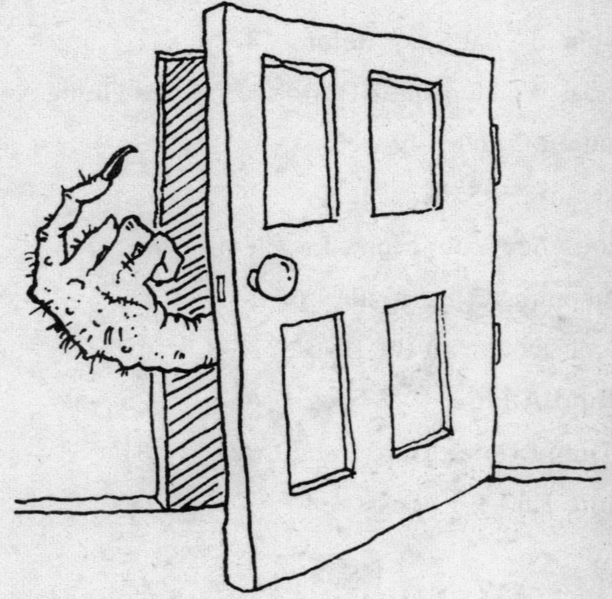

Knock, knock.
Come in.

Goose Who's Knocking at Your Door

Knock, knock.
Who's there?
Goose.
Goose who?
Goose who's knocking at your door.

Knock, knock.
Who's there?
Bet.
Bet who?
Bet you don't know who's knocking on your door!

Knock, knock.
Who's there?
Jewel.
Jewel who?
Jewel remember me when you see my face.

Knock, knock.
Who's there?
Chester.
Chester who?
Chester minute! Don't you recognise me?

Knock, knock.
Who's there?
Viola.
Viola who?
Viola sudden you don't know me?

Knock, knock.
Who's there?
Gino.
Gino who?
Gino me? Then open the door!

Knock, knock.
Who's there?
Alda.
Alda who?
Alda time you knew who it was.

Knock, knock.
Who's there?
Yacht.
Yacht who?
Yacht a know me by now.

Knock, knock.
Who's there?
Dishes.
Dishes who?
Dishes your friend, open the door.

Will you remember me in one day's time?
Of course I will.
Will you remember me in a week's time?
Of course I will.
Will you remember me in a year's time?
Of course I will.
Will you remember me in ten year's time?
Of course I will.
Knock, knock.
Who's there?
See – you've forgotten already!

Knock, knock.
Who's there?
Ammonia.
Ammonia who?
Ammonia gonna tell you once.

Knock, knock.
Who's there?
Justin.
Justin who?
Justin Quire who is at the door.

Knock, knock.
Who's there?
Gus.
Gus who?
That's what you're supposed to do.

Knock, knock.
Who's there?
Wooden Shoe.
Wooden Shoe who?
Wooden Shoe like to know!

Knock, knock.
Who's there?
Betty.
Betty who?
Betty doesn't know who I am.

Knock, knock.
Who's there?
Kent.
Kent who?
Kent you tell?

Knock, knock.
Who's there?
Noah.
Noah who?
Noah don't know who either.

Knock, knock.
Who's there?
I don't know.
I don't know who?
Neither do I, I keep telling you that.

Knock, knock.
Who's there?
Howard.
Howard who?
Howard I know?

Knock, knock.
Who's there?
Emma.
Emma who?
Emma glad you asked me that.

Knock, knock.
Who's there?
Snow.
Snow who?
Snow use, I've lost the little card with my name on it.

Knock, knock.
Who's there?
Auto.
Auto who?
Auto know, but I've forgotten.

Knock, knock.
Who's there?
Jess.
Jess who?
Jess me and my shadow.

Knock, knock.
Who's there?
One.
One who?
One-der why you keep asking that?

Knock, knock.
Who's there?
Alma.
Alma who?
Alma not going to tell you!

Knock, knock.
Who's there?
Zoom.
Zoom who?
Zoom do you expect?

Knock, knock.
Who's there?
Amy.
Amy who?
Amy fraid I've forgotten.

Knock, knock.
Who's there?
Arfur.
Arfur who?
Arfur got.

Knock, knock.
Who's there?
Ewan.
Ewan who?
No, just me.

Knock, knock.
Who's there?
Cozy.
Cozy who?
Cozy who's knocking will you?

Knock, knock.
Who's there?
Sam.
Sam who?
Sam person who knocked on the door last time.

Knock, knock.
Who's there?
Fozzie.
Fozzie who?
Fozzie hundredth time, my name is Nigel!

Knock, knock.
Who's there?
Sonia.
Sonia who?
Sonia paper-boy making a delivery.

Knock, knock.
Who's there?
Norma Lee.
Norma Lee who?
Norma Lee I don't go around knocking on doors, but you
   see I have this wonderful set of encyclopedias.

Knock, knock.
Who's there?
Gerald.
Gerald who?
Gerald friend again!

Knock, knock.
Who's there?
Spectre.
Spectre who?
Spectre Columbo. You're under arrest.

Knock, knock.
Who's there?
Diploma.
Diploma who?
Diploma to fix the leak.

Knock, knock.
Who's there?
Detail.
Detail who?
Detail-a-phone operator.

Knock, knock.
Who's there?
The Avon Lady. Your bell's broken.

Knock, knock.
Who's there?
Doctor.
Doctor who?
How did you guess?

Knock, knock.
Who's there?
Soup.
Soup who?
Soup-erman!

Knock, knock.
Who's there?
Ammonia.
Ammonia who?
Ammonia little boy who can't reach the doorbell.

Knock, knock.
Who's there?
Doctor.
Doctor who?
Doctor Foster – I've just come from Gloucester.

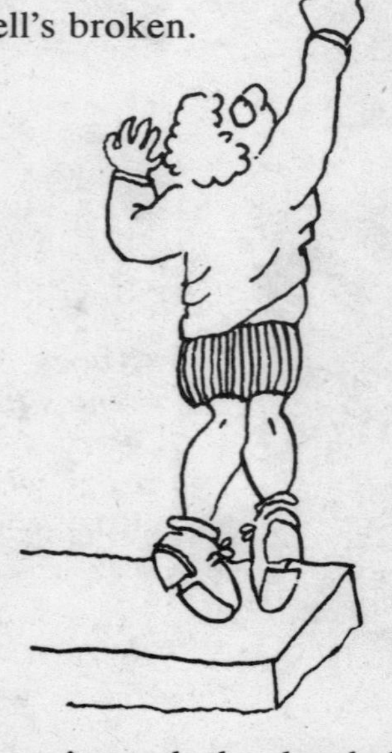

Knock, knock.
Who's there?
Ilka.
Ilka who?
Ilka-pone.

Knock, knock.
Who's there?
Cologne.
Cologne who?
Cologne Ranger is here!

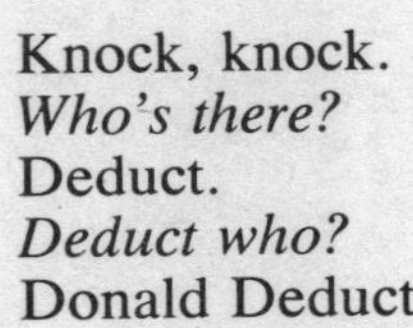

Knock, knock.
Who's there?
Ohio.
Ohio who?
Ohio Silver!

Knock, knock.
Who's there?
Deduct.
Deduct who?
Donald Deduct.

Knock, knock.
Who's there?
Sigrid.
Sigrid who?
Sigrid service – open up.

Knock, knock.
Who's there?
Scissor.
Scissor who?
Scissor and Cleopatra.

Knock, knock.
Who's there?
N.E.
N.E. who?
N.E. body you like so long as you let me in.

Knock, knock.
Who's there?
Max.
Max who?
Max no difference, just open the door.

Knock, knock.
Who's there?
Izzie.
Izzie who?
Izzie at the door? You'd better answer it then.

Knock, knock.
Who's there?
Laurie.
Laurie who?
Laurie driver.

Knock, knock.
Who's there?
Amanda.
Amanda who?
Amanda fix the television.

Wotza Name!

Knock, knock.
Who's there?
Aaron.
Aaron who?
Aaron the barber's floor.

Knock, knock.
Who's there?
Abel.
Abel who?
Abel seaman.

Knock, knock.
Who's there?
Adam.
Adam who?
Adam up and tell me the total.

Knock, knock.
Who's there?
Adelia.
Adelia who?
Adelia the cards after you cut the pack.

Knock, knock.
Who's there?
Adeline.
Adeline who?
Adeline extra to the letter.

Knock, knock.
Who's there?
Adrian.
Adrian who?
Adrian my hair 'cos it's wet.

Knock, knock.
Who's there?
Alan.
Alan who?
Alan't my lesson.

Knock, knock.
Who's there?
Aldous.
Aldous who?
Aldous who want to leave the room, put your hand up.

Knock, knock.
Who's there?
Aldous.
Aldous who?
Aldous who aren't interested – go home.

Knock, knock.
Who's there?
Alex.
Alex who?
Alex Plain later.

Knock, knock.
Who's there?
Alfie.
Alfie who?
Alfie you in my dreams.

Knock, knock.
Who's there?
Alice.
Alice who?
Alice N. Tew if you'll listen to me.

Knock, knock.
Who's there?
Alma.
Alma who?
Alma sweets have gone.

Knock, knock.
Who's there?
Althea.
Althea who?
Althea later this afternoon.

Knock, knock.
Who's there?
Amos.
Amos who?
Amos-quito bit me.

Knock, knock.
Who's there?
Andy.
Andy who?
Andy bit me again.

Knock, knock.
Who's there?
Anatole.
Anatole who?
Anatole me you're a pain in the neck.

Knock, knock.
Who's there?
Anderson.
Anderson who?
Anderson and daughter came too.

Knock, knock.
Who's there?
Andrew.
Andrew who?
Andrew a picture of Averil that hurt her feelings.

Knock, knock.
Who's there?
Andrew.
Andrew who?
Andrew all her money out of the bank.

Knock, knock.
Who's there?
Andy.
Andy who?
Andy little gadgets to have, door knockers.

Knock, knock.
Who's there?
Anita.
Anita who?
Anita you like I need a hole in the head.

Knock, knock.
Who's there?
Anna.
Anna who?
Anna going to tell you anything.

Knock, knock.
Who's there?
Anthea.
Anthea who?
Anthea get home by 8 o'clock, or else!

Knock, knock.
Who's there?
Athena.
Athena who?
Athena flying saucer.

Knock, knock.
Who's there?
Barry.
Barry who?
Barry your bone in the garden little dog.

Knock, knock.
Who's there?
Belinda.
Belinda who?
Belinda church steeple.

Knock, knock.
Who's there?
Bella.
Bella who?
Bella bottom trousers.

Knock, knock.
Who's there?
Ben.
Ben who?
Ben away a long time.

Knock, knock.
Who's there?
Bruce.
Bruce who?
I Bruce very easily, don't hit me!

Knock, knock.
Who's there?
Buster.
Buster who?
Buster the cemetary, please.

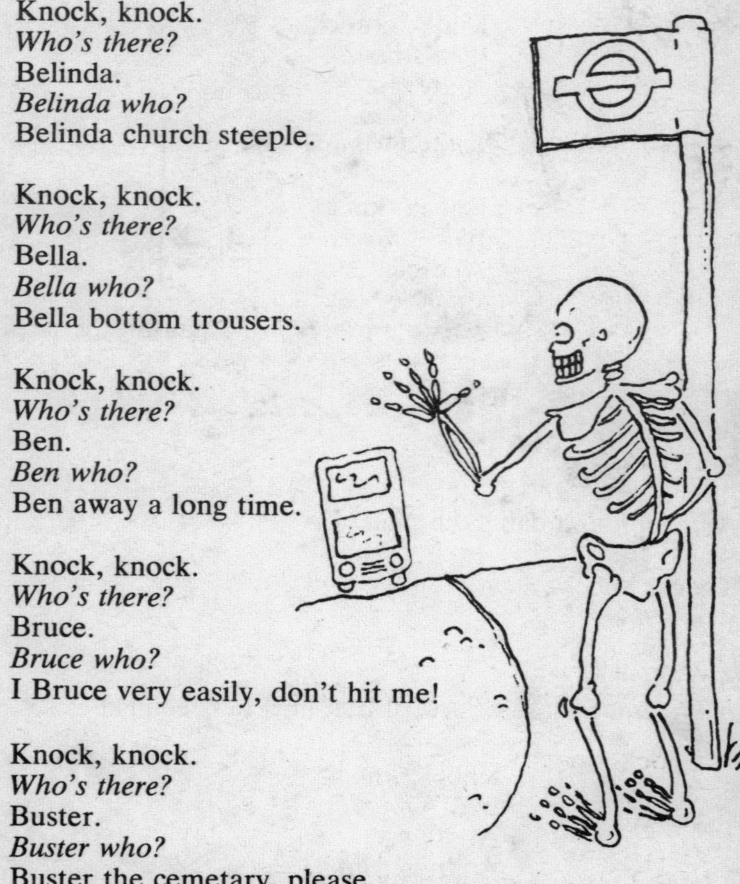

Knock, knock.
Who's there?
Buster.
Buster who?
Buster tyre, can I use your phone?

Knock, knock.
Who's there?
Carrie.
Carrie who?
Carrie me home, I'm tired.

Knock, knock.
Who's there?
Celeste.
Celeste who?
Celeste time I lend you money.

Knock, knock.
Who's there?
Chesterfield.
Chesterfield who?
Chesterfield full of cows, nothing else.

Knock, knock.
Who's there?
Colin.
Colin who?
Colin and see me on your way home.

Knock, knock.
Who's there?
Colleen.
Colleen who?
Colleen up your room, it's filthy.

Knock, knock.
Who's there?
Cynthia.
Cynthia who?
Cynthia been away so much has happened.

Knock, knock.
Who's there?
Cyril.
Cyril who?
Cyril pleasure to meet you again.

Knock, knock.
Who's there?
Daisy.
Daisy who?
Daisy plays, nights he sleeps.

Knock, knock.
Who's there?
Dana.
Dana who?
Dana talk with your mouth full.

Knock, knock.
Who's there?
Daryl.
Daryl who?
Daryl never be another you!

Knock, knock.
Who's there?
Dawn.
Dawn who?
Dawn leave me standing out here in the cold.

        Knock, knock.
        Who's there?
        Deena.
        Deena who?
        Deena hear you the first time.

Knock, knock.
Who's there?
Derek.
Derek who?
Derek of the 'Mary Rose'.

        Knock, knock.
        Who's there?
        Diana.
        Diana who?
        Diana Mals are restless, open the cage.

Knock, knock.
Who's there?
Dick.
Dick who?
Dick potatoes out of the ground.

        Knock, knock.
        Who's there?
        Dinah.
        Dinah who?
        Dinah shoot until you see the whites of their eyes.

Knock, knock.
Who's there?
Drucilla.
Drucilla who?
Drucilla kid you! You might have got hurt!

        Knock, knock.
        Who's there?
        Eddie.
        Eddie who?
        Eddie Body home?

Knock, knock.
Who's there?
Edith.
Edith who?
Edith'd me on the lipth.

        Knock, knock.
        Who's there?
        Eileen.
        Eileen who?
        Eileen over backwards to make you happy.

Knock, knock.
Who's there?
Elaine.
Elaine who?
Elaine in the country.

Knock, knock.
Who's there?
Elsie.
Elsie who?
Elsie you around.

Knock, knock.
Who's there?
Elsie.
Elsie who?
Elsie you later.

> Knock, knock.
> *Who's there?*
> Enoch.
> *Enoch who?*
> Enoch and Enoch, but nobody opens the door.

Knock, knock.
Who's there?
Ernie.
Ernie who?
Ernie plenty of money are you?

> Knock, knock.
> *Who's there?*
> Esau.
> *Esau who?*
> Esau me break the window so let me in quick.

Knock, knock.
Who's there?
Esme.
Esme who?
Esme petticoat hanging down at the back?

> Knock, knock.
> *Who's there?*
> Esther.
> *Esther who?*
> Esther anything I can do for you?

Knock, knock.
Who's there?
Eugenie.
Eugenie who?
Eugenie from the bottle will grant you three wishes.

> Knock, knock.
> *Who's there?*
> Euripedes.
> *Euripedes who?*
> Euripedes trousers and you'll pay for a new pair!

Knock, knock.
Who's there?
Eumenides.
Eumenides who?
Eumenides trousers and I won't tell that you ripped them.

> Knock, knock.
> *Who's there?*
> Eva.
> *Eva who?*
> Eva I told you, would you let me in?

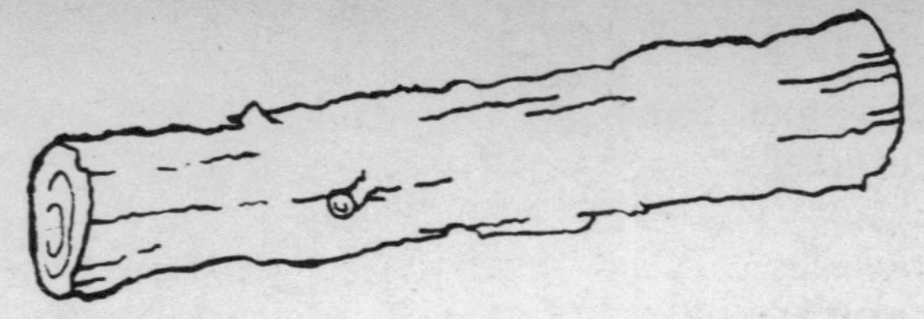

Knock, knock.
Who's there?
Eva.
Eva who?
Eva caber is what Scotsmen do at the Highland Games.

Knock, knock.
Who's there?
Evadne.
Evadne who?
Evadne problems with your teeth?

Knock, knock.
Who's there?
Evadne.
Evadne who?
Evadne snails for tea? They're horrible!

Knock, knock.
Who's there?
Ezra.
Ezra who?
Ezra no hope for me?

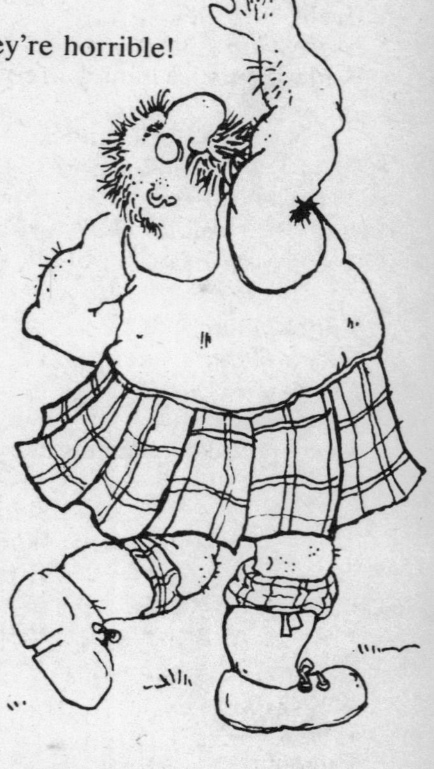

Knock, knock.
Who's there?
Fanny.
Fanny who?
Fanny body calls, I'm out.

Knock, knock.
Who's there?
Felix.
Felix who?
Felix-ited all over.

Knock, knock.
Who's there?
Fiona.
Fiona who?
Fiona of the house, I've come for the rent.

Knock, knock.
Who's there?
Fiona.
Fiona who?
Fiona had something better to do, do you think I'd hang
  around here?

Knock, knock.
Who's there?
Fitzwilliam.
Fitzwilliam who?
Fitzwilliam better than it fits me.

Knock, knock.
Who's there?
Fletcher.
Fletcher who?
Fletcher self go.

Knock, knock.
Who's there?
Frank.
Frank who?
Frankenstein.

Knock, knock.
Who's there?
Fred.
Fred who?
Fred I can't come out tonight.

Knock, knock.
Who's there?
Fred.
Fred who?
Fred I'm going to have to leave now.

Knock, knock.
Who's there?
Freddie.
Freddie who?
Freddie or not, here I come!

Knock, knock.
Who's there?
Gay.
Gay who?
Gay Topen, that's how the cows got out.

Knock, knock.
Who's there?
Gerald.
Gerald who?
Gerald washed up.

Knock, knock.
Who's there?
Gladys.
Gladys who?
Gladys E. Yew.

Knock, knock.
Who's there?
Gladys.
Gladys who?
Gladys Friday, aren't you?

Knock, knock.
Who's there?
Gretel.
Gretel who?
Gretel Long little doggie.

Knock, knock.
Who's there?
Guthrie.
Guthrie who?
Guthrie blind mice.

Knock, knock.
Who's there?
Harold.
Harold who?
Harold do you think I look?

Knock, knock.
Who's there?
Heidi Clare.
Heidi Clare who?
Heidi Clare war on you.

Knock, knock.
Who's there?
Henrietta.
Henrietta who?
Henrietta hat because he lost a bet.

Knock, knock.
Who's there?
Homer.
Homer who?
Homer gain!

Knock, knock.
Who's there?
Howard.
Howard who?
Howard you like a punch on the nose?

Knock, knock.
Who's there?
Howard.
Howard who?
Howard you like to stand out here in the cold while some
   idiot keeps saying 'Who's there?'

Knock, knock.
Who's there?
Hugh.
Hugh who?
Hugh is going to let me in then?

Knock, knock.
Who's there?
Hugo.
Hugo who?
Hugo first – I'm frightened!

Knock, knock.
Who's there?
Ida.
Ida who?
Ida know. Sorry!

Knock, knock.
Who's there?
Irma.
Irma who?
Irma big girl now.

Knock, knock.
Who's there?
Isabel.
Isabel who?
Isabel on a bike really necessary?

Knock, knock.
Who's there?
Ivan.
Ivan who?
Ivan my money back.

Knock, knock.
Who's there?
Ivan.
Ivan who?
Ivan U. Hat, do you like it?

Knock, knock.
Who's there?
Ivor.
Ivor who?
Ivor fortune.

Knock, knock.
Who's there?
Jack.
Jack who?
Jack Potts.

Knock, knock.
Who's there?
Jackson.
Jackson who?
Jackson the telephone, you'd better answer it.

Knock, knock.
Who's there?
Janet.
Janet who?
Janet has too many holes in it, the fish will escape.

Knock, knock.
Who's there?
Jeff.
Jeff who?
Jeff in one ear, shout!

Knock, knock.
Who's there?
Jethro.
Jethro who?
Jethro the boat and stop talking so much.

Knock, knock.
Who's there?
Jimmy.
Jimmy who?
Jimmy a little kiss on the cheek.

Knock, knock.
Who's there?
Joan.
Joan who?
Joan call us, we'll call you.

Knock, knock.
Who's there?
Joe Namath.
Joe Namath who?
Joe Namath not on the door, that's why I knocked.

Knock, knock.
Who's there?
John.
John who?
John me in a cup of tea.

Knock, knock.
Who's there?
Josette.
Josette who?
Josette down and be quiet.

Knock, knock.
Who's there?
Juliet.
Juliet who?
Juliet the same amount but she's ok.

Knock, knock.
Who's there?
Juno.
Juno who?
I dunno, Juno?

Knock, knock.
Who's there?
Justin.
Justin who?
Justin Casey howls, give him his bottle.

Knock, knock.
Who's there?
Justin.
Justin who?
Justin time for a cup of tea.

Knock, knock.
Who's there?
Justin.
Justin who?
Justin time for dinner.

Knock, knock.
Who's there?
Kay.
Kay who?
Kay, L, M, N, O, P, Q, R, S, T, U, V, W, X, Y, Z.

Knock, knock.
Who's there?
Kenneth.
Kenneth who?
Kenneth little kid play with you?

Knock, knock.
Who's there?
Lena.
Lena who?
Lena little closer. I want to tell you a secret.

Knock, knock.
Who's there?
Liz.
Liz who?
Lizen to me when I'm talking to you.

Knock, knock.
Who's there?
Liza.
Liza who?
Liza wrong to tell.

Knock, knock.
Who's there?
Lou.
Lou who?
Lou M.T. Now you can go in.

Knock, knock.
Who's there?
Lucretia.
Lucretia who?
Lucretia from the Black Lagoon.

Knock, knock.
Who's there?
Luke.
Luke who?
Luke and see who it is.

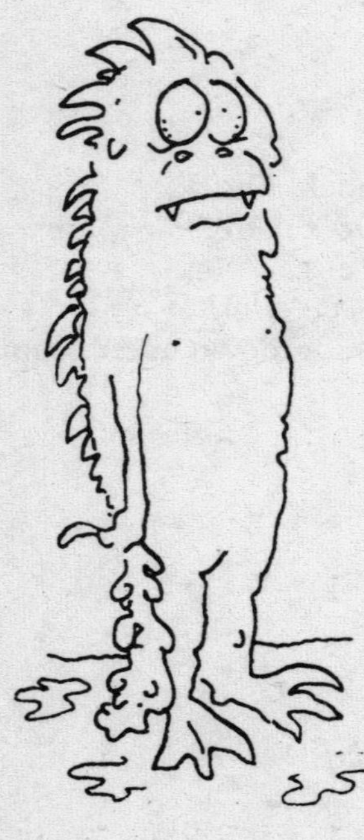

Knock, knock.
Who's there?
Luke.
Luke who?
Luke through the keyhole and see.

Knock, knock.
Who's there?
Lydia.
Lydia who?
Lydia dustbin just blew away.

Knock, knock.
Who's there?
Lydia.
Lydia who?
Lydia teapot is cracked.

Knock, knock.
Who's there?
Lyndon.
Lyndon who?
Lyndon ear and I'll tell you.

Knock, knock.
Who's there?
Mabel.
Mabel who?
Mabel doesn't ring either.

Knock, knock.
Who's there?
Mandy.
Mandy who?
Mandy guns, here come the Indians.

Knock, knock.
Who's there?
Mandy.
Mandy who?
Mandy lifeboats, we're sinking.

Knock, knock.
Who's there?
Margo.
Margo who?
Margo and fetch pa off the roof, his ladder just broke.

Knock, knock.
Who's there?
Martin.
Martin who?
Martin of peas won't open!

Knock, knock.
Who's there?
Matt.
Matt who?
Mattadore.

Knock, knock.
Who's there?
Matthew.
Matthew who?
Matthew lace has come undone.

Knock, knock.
Who's there?
Max.
Max who?
Max no difference – just open the door!

Knock, knock.
Who's there?
Michael.
Michael who?
Michael has just boiled, like a cup of tea?

Knock, knock.
Who's there?
Michelle.
Michelle who?
Michelle had a big crab inside it.

Knock, knock.
Who's there?
Mischa.
Mischa who?
Mischa a lot.

Knock, knock.
Who's there?
Morris.
Morris who?
Morris in the pot, help yourself.

Knock, knock.
Who's there?
Moses.
Moses who?
Moses will you come and have tea with us?

Knock, knock.
Who's there?
Nadya.
Nadya who?
Nadya head if you understand what I'm saying.

Knock, knock.
Who's there?
Nettie.
Nettie who?
Nettie as a fruitcake.

Knock, knock.
Who's there?
Nicholas.
Nicholas who?
Nicholas girls shouldn't climb trees.

Knock, knock.
Who's there?
Norman.
Norman who?
Norman has ever set foot here before.

Knock, knock.
Who's there?
Norman.
Norman who?
Norman invasion was 1066.

Knock, knock.
Who's there?
Odysseus.
Odysseus who?
Odysseus the final straw!

Knock, knock.
Who's there?
Olaf.
Olaf who?
Olaf if you think it's that funny!

Knock, knock.
Who's there?
Olive.
Olive who?
Olive across the road.

> Knock, knock.
> *Who's there?*
> Olive.
> *Olive who?*
> Olive just around the corner.

> > Knock, knock.
> > *Who's there?*
> > Oliver.
> > *Oliver who?*
> > Oliver nother one if you've got it.

> > Knock, knock.
> > *Who's there?*
> > Oliver.
> > *Oliver who?*
> > Oliver troubles are over.

> Knock, knock.
> *Who's there?*
> Olivia.
> *Olivia who?*
> Olivia me alone!

Knock, knock.   Knock, knock.
Who's there?   *Who's there?*
Orson.   Oscar.
Orson who?   *Oscar who?*
Orson around again?   Oscar if she wants a drink.

Knock, knock.
Who's there?
Oscar.
Oscar who?
Oscar stupid question, you get a stupid answer.

> Knock, knock.
> *Who's there?*
> Patsy.
> *Patsy who?*
> Patsy dog on the head, he likes it.

Knock, knock.
Who's there?
Paul Aidy.
Paul Aidy who?
Paul Aidy, she tripped and fell in the mud.

> > Knock, knock.
> > *Who's there?*
> > Paul.
> > *Paul who?*
> > Paul hard, the door's stuck again.

Knock, knock.
Who's there?
Phil.
Phil who?
Phil up my hot water-bottle, I'm cold.

Knock, knock.
Who's there?
Philip.
Philip who?
Philip the tank, I've got a long way to go.

Knock, knock.
Who's there?
Philippa.
Philippa who?
Philippa bath-tub, I'm dirty.

Knock, knock.
Who's there?
Phineas.
Phineas who?
Phineas thing happened to me on the way here.

Knock, knock.
Who's there?
Phoebe.
Phoebe who?
Phoebe too high for us to pay.

Knock, knock.
Who's there?
Phyllis.
Phyllis who?
Phyllis in on the news.

Knock, knock.
Who's there?
Ralph.
Ralph who?
Ralph! Ralph! Ralph! I'm your puppy-dog.

Knock, knock.
Who's there?
Robin.
Robin who?
Robin the larder is wrong.

Knock, knock.
Who's there?
Romeo.
Romeo who?
Romeo Ver to the other side of the lake.

Knock, knock.
Who's there?
Rosa.
Rosa who?
Rosa carrots grow in our garden.

Knock, knock.
Who's there?
Roxanne.
Roxanne who?
Roxanne pebbles are all over this beach.

Knock, knock.
Who's there?
Rufus.
Rufus who?
Rufus quick, we're getting wet.

Knock, knock.
Who's there?
Russell.
Russell who?
Russell up something to eat.

Knock, knock.
Who's there?
Sacha.
Sacha who?
Sacha lot of fuss about nothing.

Knock, knock.
Who's there?
Sadie.
Sadie who?
Sadie ten times table twice.

Knock, knock.
Who's there?
Seth.
Seth who?
Seth me, and what I seth goes.

Knock, knock.
Who's there?
Seymour.
Seymour who?
Seymour if you have a pane of glass in your door.

Knock, knock.
Who's there?
Shelly.
Shelly who?
Shelly Con Carne, a Mexican dish.

Knock, knock.
Who's there?
Sonya.
Sonya who?
Sonya foot, I can smell it from here.

Knock, knock.
Who's there?
Stan.
Stan who?
Stan back, I'm coming through.

Knock, knock.
Who's there?
Stefan.
Stefan who?
Stefan it quick!

Knock, knock.
Who's there?
Stefan.
Stefan who?
Stefan Nonsense.

Knock, knock.
Who's there?
Stella.
Stella who?
Stella no answer at the door.

Knock, knock.
Who's there?
Tamara.
Tamara who?
Tamara the world!

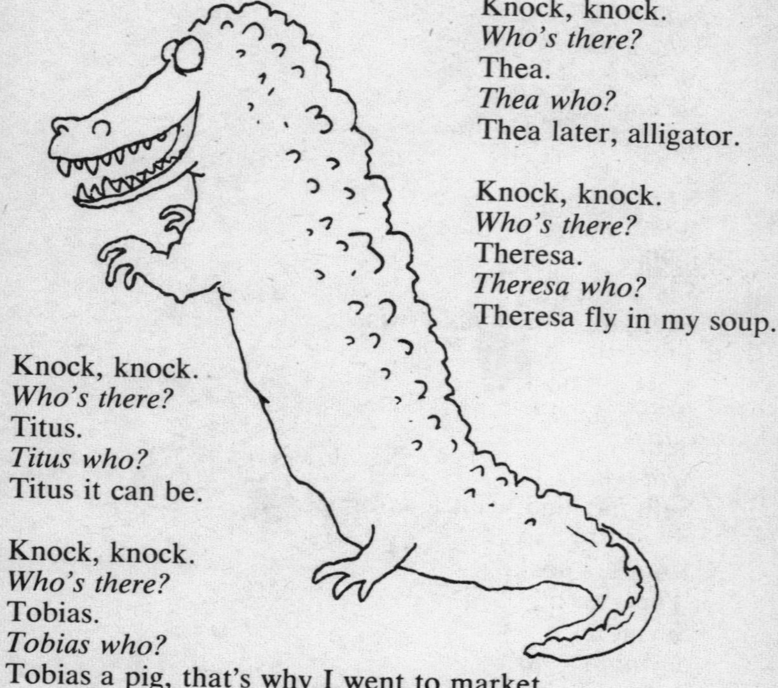

Knock, knock.
Who's there?
Thea.
Thea who?
Thea later, alligator.

Knock, knock.
Who's there?
Theresa.
Theresa who?
Theresa fly in my soup.

Knock, knock.
Who's there?
Titus.
Titus who?
Titus it can be.

Knock, knock.
Who's there?
Tobias.
Tobias who?
Tobias a pig, that's why I went to market.

Knock, knock.
Who's there?
Tyrone.
Tyrone who?
Tyrone shoelaces, you're old enough.

Knock, knock.
Who's there?
Uriah.
Uriah who?
Keep Uriah on the ball.

Knock, knock.
Who's there?
Violet.
Violet who?
Violet the cat out of the bag?

Knock, knock.
Who's there?
Waldo.
Waldo who?
Waldo the washing up in the morning.

Knock, knock.
Who's there?
Warren.
Warren who?
Warren my birthday suit.

Knock, knock.
Who's there?
Warren.
Warren who?
Warren peace is a famous Russian novel.

Knock, knock.
Who's there?
Wayne.
Wayne who?
Wayne are you coming over to my house?

> Knock, knock.
> *Who's there?*
> Wendy.
> *Wendy who?*
> Wendy go? I never saw him.

Knock, knock.
Who's there?
William.
William who?
William Eynd my bike while I go to the shops?

Knock, knock.
Who's there?
William.
William who?
William mind your own business!

> Knock, knock.
> *Who's there?*
> Wilma.
> *Wilma who?*
> Wilma dreams come true?

Knock, knock.
Who's there?
Willis.
Willis who?
Willis rain never end?

> Knock, knock.
> *Who's there?*
> Willy.
> *Willy who?*
> Willy make it? I bet he won't!

Knock, knock.
Who's there?
Yolande.
Yolande who?
Yolande me a pound, I'll pay you back next week.

> Knock, knock.
> *Who's there?*
> Zena.
> *Zena who?*
> Zena stealing my books.

> Knock, knock.
> *Who's there?*
> Zenia.
> *Zenia who?*
> Zenia on TV in that commercial.

Aries a Reason Why I Talk This Way

Knock, knock.
Who's there?
Aries.
Aries who?
Aries a reason why I talk this way.

Knock, knock.
Who's there?
Adolf.
Adolf who?
Adolf ball hit me in the mouth, that's why I talk like this.

Knock, knock.
Who's there?
Thayer.
Thayer who?
Thayer thorry and I won't throw thisth pie in your fathe.

Knock, knock.
Who's there?
Dorrie.
Dorrie who?
Dorrie I updet you.

Knock, knock.
Who's there?
Canoe.
Canoe who?
Canoe come out and play with me?

Knock, knock.
Who's there?
Dwayne.
Dwayne who?
Dwayne the bath-tub. I'm dwowning.

Knock, knock.
Who's there?
Sibyl.
Sibyl who?
Sibyl Simon met a pieman going to the fair.

Knock, knock.
Who's there?
Athol.
Athol who?
Athol'd my bike, tho I had to walk.

Knock, knock.
Who's there?
Oswald.
Oswald who?
Oswald by bubble gum.

Knock, knock.
Who's there?
Zephyr.
Zephyr who?
Zephyr de doctor, I got a code id de node.

Knock, knock.
Who's there?
Twain.
Twain who?
Twains are what wabbits take a twip on.

Knock, knock.
Who's there?
Wayne.
Wayne who?
Wayne is coming through the roof.

Knock, knock.
Who's there?
Lief.
Lief who?
Lief me alone.

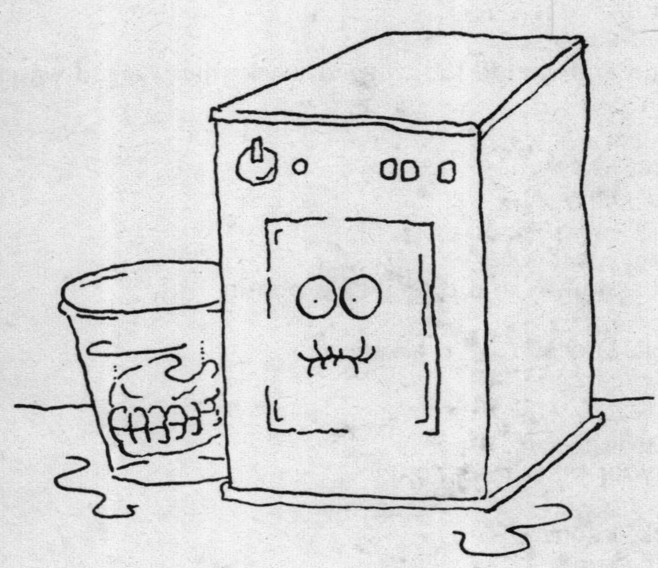

Knock, knock.
Who's there?
Dishwasher.
Dishwasher who?
Dishwasher the way I spoke before I had false teeth.

Knock, knock.
Who's there?
Bruce.
Bruce who?
I Bruce very easily.

Knock, knock.
Who's there?
Toothy.
Toothy who?
Toothy ith the day before Wednethday.

Knock, knock.
Who's there?
Beth.
Beth who?
Beth wisheth, thweetie!

Knock, knock.
Who's there?
Althea.
Althea who?
Althea later in the afternoon.

Knock, knock.
Who's there?
Dishes.
Dishes who?
Dishes your friend Margaret, so open the door.

Knock, knock.
Who's there?
Dishwasher.
Dishwasher who?
Dishwashn't de way I shpoke before I had falsh teeth!

Knock, knock.
Who's there?
Wound.
Wound who?
Wound and wound the wugged wocks the wagged wascal
    wan.

Knock, knock.
Who's there?
Passion.
Passion who?
Just Passion by and thought I'd pop in.

Knock, knock.
Who's there?
Puss.
Puss who?
Puss your bike, it's safer.

Knock, knock.
Who's there?
Matthew.
Matthew who?
Matthew is pinching my foot.

Knock–Knock Dictionary

Knock, knock.
Who's there?
Alec.
Alec who?
Alec-tricity is shocking.

Knock, knock.
Who's there?
Algy.
Algy who?
Algy-bra.

Knock, knock.
Who's there?
Alma.
Alma who?
Alma-nack.

Knock, knock.
Who's there?
Amsterdam.
Amsterdam who?
Amsterdam is like plum jam, but made from hamsters.

Knock, knock.
Who's there?
Anna.
Anna who?
Anna-tomical.

Knock, knock.
Who's there?
Annie.
Annie who?
Annie-versary.

Knock, knock.
Who's there?
Ann.
Ann who?
Ann-onymous.

Knock, knock.
Who's there?
Arthur.
Arthur who?
Arthur-itis, it's very painful.

Knock, knock.
Who's there?
Arthur.
Arthur who?
Arthur-mometer is good for measuring the temperature.

Knock, knock.
Who's there?
Bab.
Bab who?
Bab Boone is a real ape.

Knock, knock.
Who's there?
Bart.
Bart who?
Bart-enders serve drinks.

Knock, knock.
Who's there?
Bill.
Bill who?
Bill-tup area.

Knock, knock.
Who's there?
Bison.
Bison who?
Pudding Bison.

Knock, knock.
Who's there?
Cameron.
Cameron who?
Cameron film are needed to take pictures.

Knock, knock.
Who's there?
Cargo.
Cargo who?
Cargo 'beep beep'.

Knock, knock.
Who's there?
Clarkeson.
Clarkeson who?
Clarkeson watches tell the time.

Knock, knock.
Who's there?
Dan.
Dan who?
Dan Druff.

Knock, knock.
Who's there?
Della.
Della who?
Della-katessen.

Knock, knock.
Who's there?
Denial.
Denial who?
Denial's a river in Egypt.

Knock, knock.
Who's there?
Dmitri.
Dmitri who?
Dmitri is where lamb chops grow.

Knock, knock.
Who's there?
Harris.
Harris who?
Harris nice to have on the top of your head.

Knock, knock.
Who's there?
Horace.
Horace who?
Horace-scopes can be fun.

Knock, knock.
Who's there?
Lass.
Lass who?
That's what cowboys use, isn't it?

Knock, knock.
Who's there?
Maxie.
Maxie who?
Maxie-mum.

Knock, knock.
Who's there?
Mike.
Mike who?
Mike-robe.

Knock, knock.
Who's there?
Minnie.
Minnie who?
Minnie-mum.

Knock, knock.
Who's there?
Miss.
Miss who?
Miss L. Toe is nice at Christmas.

Knock, knock.
Who's there?
Nick.
Nick who?
Nick R. Elastic.

Knock, knock.
Who's there?
Orson.
Orson who?
Orson cart.

Knock, knock.
Who's there?
Tennis.
Tennis who?
Tennis the sum of five plus five.

Knock, knock.
Who's there?
Tilly.
Tilly who?
Tilly-vision is my favourite invention.

Knock, knock.
Who's there?
Tish.
Tish who?
That's good for blowing your nose.

Knock, knock.
Who's there?
Tuba.
Tuba who?
Tuba toothpaste.

Knock, knock.
Who's there?
Walter.
Walter who?
Walter wall carpets.

Knock, knock.
Who's there?
X.
X who?
X can be boiled for breakfast.

Knock, knock.
Who's there?
Zombies.
Zombies who?
Zombies make honey, others are queens.

That's a Big Word!

Knock, knock.
Who's there?
Allocate.
Allocate who?
Allocate, how are you dear?

Knock, knock.
Who's there?
Armageddon.
Armageddon who?
Armageddon out of here!

Knock, knock.
Who's there?
Audacity.
Audacity who?
Audacity way to be.

Knock, knock.
Who's there?
Bigotry.
Bigotry who?
Bigotry than the one in your garden.

Knock, knock.
Who's there?
Census.
Census who?
Census Saturday we don't have to go to school.

Knock, knock.
Who's there?
Denial.
Denial who?
Denial's in Egypt, but I'm here.

Knock, knock.
Who's there?
Diesel.
Diesel who?
Diesel teach you to go around knocking on doors.

Knock, knock.
Who's there?
Dimension.
Dimension who?
Dimension it!

Knock, knock.
Who's there?
Dinamite.
Dinamite who?
Dinamite if you ask her nicely.

Knock, knock.
Who's there?
Dinosaur.
Dinosaur who?
Dinosaur with you because you called her stupid.

Knock, knock.
Who's there?
Disaster.
Disaster who?
Disaster be my lucky day.

Knock, knock.
Who's there?
Disc.
Disc who?
Disc is a recorded message . . .

Knock, knock.
Who's there?
Disease.
Disease who?
Disease clothes fit you?

Knock, knock.
Who's there?
Disguise.
Disguise who?
Disguise the limit!

Knock, knock.
Who's there?
Dismay.
Dismay who?
Dismay be a joke but it doesn't make me laugh!

Knock, knock.
Who's there?
Element.
Element who?
Element to tell you that she can't see you today.

Knock, knock.
Who's there?
Formosa.
Formosa who?
Formosa the Summer I was away on my holiday.

Knock, knock.
Who's there?
Furlow.
Furlow who?
Furlow the leader.

Knock, knock.
Who's there?
Grammar.
Grammar who?
Grammar is in the Old Peoples' Home.

Knock, knock.
Who's there?
Halibut.
Halibut who?
Halibut letting me in on the secret?

Knock, knock.
Who's there?
Hijack.
Hijack who?
Hijack, how's Jill?

Knock, knock.
Who's there?
Irrigation.
Irrigation who?
Irrigation is when you need to scratch.

Knock, knock.
Who's there?
Island.
Island who?
Island on your roof with my parachute.

Knock, knock.
Who's there?
Ivory.
Ivory who?
Ivory strong, like Tarzan.

Knock, knock.
Who's there?
Laziness.
Laziness who?
Laziness bed all day, when he should be at school.

Knock, knock.
Who's there?
Mica.
Mica who?
Mica is double-parked, so hurry up!

Knock, knock.
Who's there?
Miniature.
Miniature who?
Miniature open you mouth you put your foot in it.

Knock, knock.
Who's there?
Nuisance.
Nuisance who?
What's Nuisance yesterday?

Knock, knock.
Who's there?
Ocelot.
Ocelot who?
Ocelot of questions, don't you?

Knock, knock.
Who's there?
Pharoah.
Pharoah who?
Pharoah-nuff.

Knock, knock.
Who's there?
Sheik.
Sheik who?
Sheik-speare married an Avon lady

Knock, knock.
Who's there?
Sultan.
Sultan who?
Sultan Pepper.

Knock, knock.
Who's there?
Thermos.
Thermos who?
Thermos be a better knock-knock joke than this.

Knock, knock.
Who's there?
Unite.
Unite who?
Unite a person, you call him Sir.

Knock, knock.
Who's there?
Virtue.
Virtue who?
Virtue get those big brown eyes?

Knock, knock.
Who's there?
Wanda.
Wanda who?
Wanda buy a cheap bike? It's got no wheels but . . .

Knock, knock.
Who's there?
Zone.
Zone who?
Zone shadow scares him.

Typhoid That Song Before

Knock, knock.
Who's there?
Typhoid.
Typhoid who?
Typhoid that song before.

        Knock, knock.
        Who's there?
        Weasel.
        Weasel who?
        Weasel while you work.

Knock, knock.
Who's there?
Wendy.
Wendy who?
Wendy red, red robin comes bob, bob, bobbin' along.

        Knock, knock.
        Who's there?
        Igloo.
        Igloo who?
        Igloo knew Suzie, like I know Suzie . . .

Knock, knock.
Who's there?
Amahl.
Amahl who?
Amahl shook up.

        Knock, knock.
        Who's there?
        Mia.
        Mia who?
        Mia and my shadow.

Knock, knock.
Who's there?
Noah.
Noah who?
Noah Body knows the trouble I've seen.

        Knock, knock.
        Who's there?
        Rocky.
        Rocky who?
        Rocky bye baby on the tree top.

Knock, knock.
Who's there?
Ammonia.
Ammonia who?
Ammonia a poor little sparrow . . .

Knock, knock.
Who's there?
Bridget.
Bridget who?
London Bridget falling down.

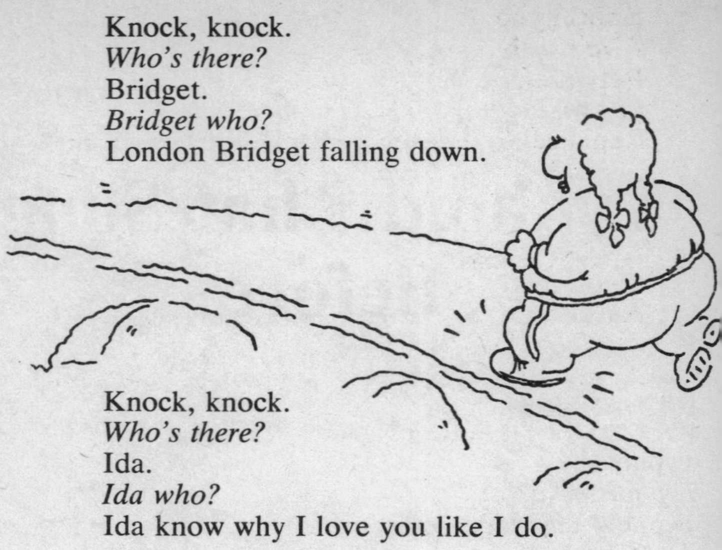

Knock, knock.
Who's there?
Ida.
Ida who?
Ida know why I love you like I do.

Knock, knock.
Who's there?
Caesar.
Caesar who?
Ceaser jolly good fellow.

Knock, knock.
Who's there?
Honda.
Honda who?
Honda the spreading chestnut tree.

Knock, knock.
Who's there?
Barbara.
Barbara who?
Barbara black sheep, have you any wool?

Knock, knock.
Who's there?
Sam and Janet.
Sam and Janet who?
Sam and Janet evening, you will meet a stranger . . .

Knock, knock.
Who's there?
A Fred.
A Fred who?
Who's a Fred of the Big Bad Wolf?

Knock, knock.
Who's there?
Heifer.
Heifer who?
Heifer sixpence is better than half a penny . . .

Knock, knock.
Who's there?
Ina Clare.
Ina Clare who?
Ina Clare day you can see forever.

Knock, knock.
Who's there?
Demon.
Demon who?
Demons are a ghoul's best friend.

Knock, knock.
Who's there?
Rapunzel.
Rapunzel who?
Rapunzel troubles in your old kitbag and smile, smile,
   smile.

Knock, knock.
Who's there?
Aardvark.
Aardvark who?
Aardvark a million miles for one of your smiles, my
   Mammy.

Knock, knock.
Who's there?
Kaye.
Kaye who?
Kaye sera sera.

Knock, knock.
Who's there?
Darren.
Darren who?
Darren young man on the flying trapeze.

Knock, knock.
Who's there?
Donna.
Donna who?
Donna sit under the apple tree with anyone else but me.

Knock, knock.
Who's there?
Butcher.
Butcher who?
Butcher left leg in, your left leg out . . .

Knock, knock.
Who's there?
Shelby.
Shelby who?
Shelby coming round the mountain when she comes.

Knock, knock.
Who's there?
Sal.
Sal who?
Sal-ong way to Tipperary . . .

Knock, knock.
Who's there?
Iguana.
Iguana who?
Iguana hold your hand.

Knock, knock.
Who's there?
Vaughan.
Vaughan who?
Vaughan day my prince vill come.

Knock, knock.
Who's there?
Donald.
Donald who?
Donald come baby, cradle and all.

Knock, knock.
Who's there?
Mayonnaise.
Mayonnaise who?
Mayonnaise have seen the glory of the coming of the Lord.

Knock, knock.
Who's there?
Hannah.
Hannah who?
Hannah partridge in a pear tree.

Knock, knock.
Who's there?
Hey.
Hey who?
Hey ho, hey ho, it's off to work we go.

Knock, knock.
Who's there?
Vera.
Vera who?
Vera all the flowers gone.

Knock, knock.
Who's there?
Cecil.
Cecil who?
Cecil have music wherever she goes.

Knock, knock.
Who's there?
Donna Mae.
Donna Mae who?
Donna Mae Kew an offer you can't refuse.

Knock, knock.
Who's there?
Sonia.
Sonia who?
Sonia bird in a gilded cage.

Knock, knock.
Who's there?
Weevil.
Weevil who?
Weevil work it out.

Knock, knock.
Who's there?
Hywel.
Hywel who?
Hywel never walk alone.

Midas Well Open the Door 'cos I'm Not Going Away!

Knock, knock.
Who's there?
Midas.
Midas who?
Midas well open the door 'cos I'm not going away.

Knock, knock.
Who's there?
Jennie.
Jennie who?
Jennie-d any help opening the door?

Knock, knock.
Who's there?
Ivan.
Ivan who?
Ivan idea you don't want to see me.

Knock, knock.
Who's there?
Fanny.
Fanny who?
Fanny body gonna open this door then?

Knock, knock.
Who's there?
Eileen.
Eileen who?
Eileen Don your bell and broke it.

Knock, knock.
Who's there?
Fanny.
Fanny who?
Fanny the way you keep saying 'Who's there?' every time I
    knock!

Knock, knock.
Who's there?
Howard.
Howard who?
Howard you know unless you open the door?

Knock, knock.
Who's there?
Anna.
Anna who?
Anna Nother thing, how many times do I have to knock on
    this door before you open up?

Knock, knock.
Who's there?
Dishes.
Dishes who?
Dishes getting boring!

Knock, knock.
Who's there?
Lettuce.
Lettuce who?
Lettuce in, won't you?

Knock, knock.
Who's there?
Ivor.
Ivor who?
Ivor sore hand from knocking on your door!

Knock, knock.
Who's there?
Luke.
Luke who?
Luke through the keyhole and you'll see.

Knock, knock.
Who's there?
Isabel.
Isabel who?
Isabel broken, 'cos I had to knock?!

Knock, knock.
Who's there?
Mavis.
Mavis who?
Mavis be the last time I knock on this door.

Knock, knock.
Who's there?
Thistle.
Thistle who?
Thistle be the last time I knock on this door.

Knock, knock.
Who's there?
Eggs.
Eggs who?
Eggstremely cold waiting for you to open the door.

Knock, knock.
Who's there?
Waddle.
Waddle who?
Waddle you give me to go away?

Knock, knock.
Who's there?
Heywood, Hugh, Harry.
Heywood, Hugh, Harry who?
Heywood Hugh Harry up and open this door.

Knock, knock.
Who's there?
Dozen.
Dozen who?
Dozen anyone live here anymore?

Knock, knock.
Who's there?
Des.
Des who?
Des no bell, dat's why I'm knocking.

Knock, knock.
Who's there?
Hobbit.
Hobbit who?
Hobbit letting me in then?

> Knock, knock.
> *Who's there?*
> Darwin.
> *Darwin who?*
> I'll be Darwin you open the door.

>> Knock, knock.
>> *Who's there?*
>> Havelock.
>> *Havelock who?*
>> Havelock put on your door.

Knock, knock.
Who's there?
Tillie.
Tillie who?
Tillie comes I'm going to wait here.

> Knock, knock.
> *Who's there?*
> Olga.
> *Olga who?*
> Olga home if you don't open up.

>> Knock, knock.
>> *Who's there?*
>> Juan.
>> *Juan who?*
>> Juan of these days you'll find out!

Knock, knock.
Who's there?
Earl.
Earl who?
Earl be glad to tell you if you open the door.

> Knock, knock.
> *Who's there?*
> Eliza.
> *Eliza who?*
> Eliza wake at night thinking about this door.

Knock, knock.
Who's there?
Isabella.
Isabella who?
Isabella dropped off so you not hear?

> Knock, knock.
> *Who's there?*
> Abbot.
> *Abbot who?*
> Abbot time you opened this door!

>> Knock, knock.
>> *Who's there?*
>> Xavier.
>> *Xavier who?*
>> Xavier breath, I'm not leaving.

Knock, knock.
Who's there?
Ferdie.
Ferdie who?
Ferdie last time, open the door!

Knock, knock.
Who's there?
Avon.
Avon who?
Avon to get in.

Tap, tap.
Who's there?
Hurd.
Hurd who?
Hurd my hand, so I couldn't knock-knock.

Knock, knock.
Who's there?
Harry.
Harry who?
Harry up and let me in!

Knock, knock.
Who's there?
Don.
Don who?
Don mess about, just open the door.

Knock, knock.
Who's there?
Doris.
Doris who?
Doris dropping off its hinges with all this knocking.

Knock, knock.
Who's there?
Savannah.
Savannah who?
Savannah you going to open the door?

Knock, knock.
Who's there?
Sis.
Sis who?
Sis any way to treat a friend?

Knock, knock.
Who's there?
Ammonia.
Ammonia who?
Ammonia gonna tell you once.

Knock, knock.
Who's there?
Isadore.
Isadore who?
Isadore open or locked?

Knock, knock.
Who's there?
Theodore.
Theodore who?
Theodore wasn't open so I knocked-knocked.

Knock, knock.
Who's there?
Ken.
Ken who?
Ken I come in?

Knock, knock.
Who's there?
Justice.
Justice who?
Justice I thought – no one at home.

Knock, knock; ting-a-ling.
Who's there?
UCI.
UCI who?
UCI had to ring because you didn't answer when I
  knocked.

Knock, knock.
Who's there?
Sincerely.
Sincerely who?
Sincerely this morning I've been waiting for you to open
  this door.

Knock, knock.
Who's there?
Lucinda.
Lucinda who?
Lucinda chain, I want to get in.

Knock, knock.
Who's there?
Adore.
Adore who?
Adore stands between us, open up!

Knock, knock.
Who's there?
Usher.
Usher who?
Usher wish you would let me in.

Knock, knock.
Who's there?
Martini.
Martini who?
Martini hand is frozen so let me in!

Knock, knock.
Who's there?
Betty.
Betty who?
Betty things to do than stand here, you know.

Knock, knock.
Who's there?
Freighter.
Freighter who?
Freighter open the door?

Knock, knock.
Who's there?
Stan.
Stan who?
Stan back, I'm knocking the door down.

Knock, knock.
Who's there?
Dozen.
Dozen who?
Dozen anyone want to let me in?

Knock, knock.
Who's there?
Stepfather.
Stepfather who?
One stepfather and I'll be in.

Knock, knock.
Who's there?
You.
You who?
You who! Is there anybody in?

Knock, knock.
Who's there?
Ken.
Ken who?
Ken you open the door and let me in?

Knock, knock.
Who's there?
Owen.
Owen who?
Owen are you going to let me in?

Knock, knock.
Who's there?
Emmett.
Emmett who?
Emmett the back door, not the front.

Knock, knock.
Who's there?
Olga.
Olga who?
Olga way when I'm good and ready.

Knock, knock.
Who's there?
Sarah.
Sarah who?
Sarah 'nother way into this building?

Knock, knock.
Who's there?
Ice cream.
Ice cream who?
Ice cream if you don't let me in.

Knock, knock.
Who's there?
Howell.
Howell who?
Howell I get in if you don't open the door.

Knock, knock.
Who's there?
Lettuce.
Lettuce who?
Lettuce in, won't you?

Knock, knock.
Who's there?
Ali.
Ali who?
Ali-luyah, at last you've opened the door.

Norma Lee I Wouldn't Have Troubled You, But . . .

Knock, knock.
Who's there?
Norma Lee.
Norma Lee who?
Norma Lee I wouldn't have troubled you, but I need help.

Knock, knock.
Who's there?
Mister.
Mister who?
Mister last bus home.

    Knock, knock.
    Who's there?
    Anne.
    Anne who?
    Anne apple just fell on my head.

        Knock, knock.
        Who's there?
        Mickey.
        Mickey who?
        Mickey's stuck in the lock!

Knock, knock.
Who's there?
Police.
Police who?
Police open the door, I have to go to the bathroom.

    Knock, knock.
    Who's there?
    Madam.
    Madam who?
    Madam finger's caught in the door.

        Knock, knock.
        Who's there?
        Musket.
        Musket who?
        Musket in, it's urgent.

Knock, knock.
Who's there?
Butter.
Butter who?
Butter be quick, I have to go to the bathroom.

    Knock, knock.
    Who's there?
    Mickey.
    Mickey who?
    Mickey dropped down the drain.

        Knock, knock.
        Who's there?
        Doris.
        Doris who?
        Doris jammed again.

Knock, knock.
Who's there?
Yelp.
Yelp who?
Yelp me! My nose is stuck in the keyhole.

Knock, knock.
Who's there?
Scold.
Scold who?
Scold outside.

Knock, knock.
Who's there?
Gutter.
Gutter who?
Gutter get in, it's snowing out here.

Knock, knock.
Who's there?
Ken.
Ken who?
Ken I Cummin, it's freezing out here?

Knock, knock.
Who's there?
Diana.
Diana who?
Diana thirst, can I have some water please?

Knock, knock.
Who's there?
Doris.
Doris who?
Doris slammed on my finger so open it quick.

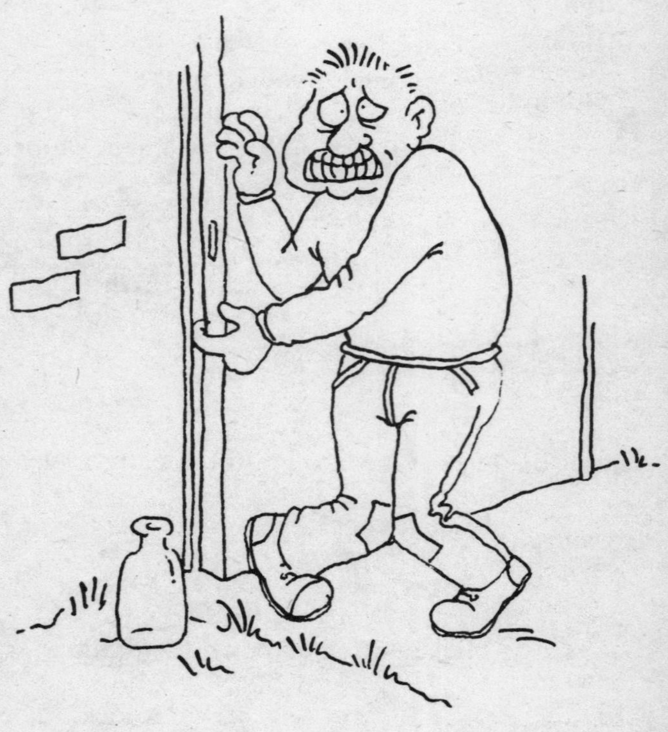

Lauren Order

Knock, knock.
Who's there?
Lauren.
Lauren who?
Lauren order.

Knock, knock.
Who's there?
Dwight.
Dwight who?
Dwight way and a wrong way.

Knock, knock.
Who's there?
Faye.
Faye who?
Faye Kearings.

Knock, knock.
Who's there?
Wanda.
Wanda who?
Wanda around while I climb through the window.

Knock, knock.
Who's there?
Ammon.
Ammon who?
Ammon old hand at picking locks.

Knock, knock.
Who's there?
Robin.
Robin who?
Robin the piggy bank again.

Knock, knock.
Who's there?
Barry.
Barry who?
Barry the treasure where no one will find it.

Knock, knock.
Who's there?
Razor.
Razor who?
Razor hands – this is a stick-up!

Knock, knock.
Who's there?
Andrew.
Andrew who?
Andrew all over the wall, and boy is she in big trouble.

Knock, knock.
Who's there?
Stop-watch.
Stop-watch who?
Stop-watch you're doing this instant!

Knock, knock.
Who's there?
Colleen.
Colleen who?
Colleen all cars!

Knock, knock.
Who's there?
Dishes.
Dishes who?
Dishes the police, open up!

Knock, knock.
Who's there?
Iris.
Iris who?
Iris Tew in the name of the law.

Knock, knock.
Who's there?
Quiet Tina.
Quiet Tina who?
Quiet Tina court room please.

Knock, knock.
Who's there?
Viscount.
Viscount who?
Viscount you behave yourself?

Knock, knock.
Who's there?
Lionel.
Lionel who?
Lionel get you nowhere, better tell the truth.

Knock, knock.
Who's there?
Delores.
Delores who?
Delores on the side of good people.

Knock, knock.
Who's there?
Geordie.
Geordie who?
Geordie-rectly to jail, do not pass go, do not collect
    £200 . . .

Knock, knock.
Who's there?
Kermit.
Kermit who?
Kermit a crime and you'll get locked up.

Knock, knock.
Who's there?
Lady.
Lady who?
Lady law down.

Knock, knock.
Who's there?
Sinbad.
Sinbad who?
Sinbad and you'll never go to Heaven.

Knock, knock.
Who's there?
Toyota.
Toyota who?
Toyota be a law against knock-knock jokes.

Bonanza!

Knock, knock.
Who's there?
Lettuce.
Lettuce who?
Lettuce tell you a few good knock-knock jokes.

Knock, knock.
Who's there?
Izzy.
Izzy who?
Izzy come, izzy go.

Knock, knock.
Who's there?
Omar.
Omar who?
Omar goodness gracious! Wrong door!

Knock, knock.
Who's there?
Odette.
Odette who?
Odette's a bad sign.

Knock, knock.
Who's there?
Les.
Les who?
Les go out for a picnic.

Knock, knock.
Who's there?
Says.
Says who?
Says me, that's who!

Knock, knock.
Who's there?
Knock, knock.
Who's there?
Knock, knock.
Who's there?
Knock, knock.
Who's there?
I'm sorry, but my mother doesn't allow me to speak
to strangers.

Knock, knock.
Who's there?
An author.
An author who?
An author joke like this and I'm off!

Knock, knock.
Who's there?
Pill.
Pill who?
Yes please, and a sheet to go with it.

Knock, knock.
Who's there?
Doughnut.
Doughnut who?
Doughnut open your presents until Christmas Day.

Knock, knock.
Who's there?
Donalette.
Donalette who?
Donalette the bed bugs bite.

Knock, knock.
Who's there?
Abba.
Abba who?
Abba banana.

Knock, knock.
Who's there?
Duck.
Duck who?
Just duck! They're throwing things at us.

Knock, knock.
Who's there?
Gorilla.
Gorilla who?
Gorilla cheese sandwich for me and I'll be right over.

Knock, knock.
Who's there?
Cassette.
Cassette who?
Cassette your dinner, I'm sorry.

Knock, knock.
Who's there?
Hammond.
Hammond who?
Hammond cheese on toast, please.

Knock, knock.
Who's there?
Amanda.
Amanda who?
Amanda-rin orange.

Knock, knock.
Who's there?
Fido.
Fido who?
Fido I have to wait here?

Knock, knock.
Who's there?
Bernadette.
Bernadette who?
Bernadette all my dinner.

Knock, knock.
Who's there?
Tank.
Tank who?
You're welcome.

Knock, knock.
Who's there?
House.
House who?
Oh, Hugh's fine thank you.

Knock, knock.
Who's there?
Pencil.
Pencil who?
Your Pencil fall down if the elastic goes.

Knock, knock.
Who's there?
Eyes.
Eyes who?
Eyes got loads more knock-knock jokes for you.

Knock, knock.
Who's there?
P.
P. who?
P. Nuts are an elephant's favourite treat.

Knock, knock.
Who's there?
Who.
Who who?
Bad echo in here, isn't there!

Knock, knock.
Who's there?
Pizza.
Pizza who?
Pizza cake would be great right now.

Knock, knock.
Who's there?
Closure.
Closure who?
Closure mouth when you eat.

Knock, knock.
Who's there?
Nora.
Nora who?
Nora Bone.

Knock, knock.
Who's there?
General Lee.
General Lee who?
General Lee I don't mind school dinners.

Knock, knock.
Who's there?
Alec.
Alec who?
Alec coffee, but I don't like tea.

Knock, knock.
Who's there?
Harriet.
Harriet who?
Harriet all my lunch, I'm starving.

Knock, knock.
Who's there?
Gorilla.
Gorilla who?
Gorilla me a hamburger.

Knock, knock.
Who's there?
Wooden.
Wooden who?
Wooden you like to know.

Knock, knock.
Who's there?
Punch.
Punch who?
Not me, please!

Knock, knock.
Who's there?
Boo.
Boo who?
Just boo! I'm a ghost.

Ring! Ring!
Who's there?
Hurd my.
Hurd my who?
Hurd my hand so I can't knock.

Knock, knock.
Who's there?
One-eye.
One-eye who?
You're the One-eye care for.

Knock, knock.
Who's there?
Jupiter.
Jupiter who?
Jupiter hurry, or you'll miss the bus.

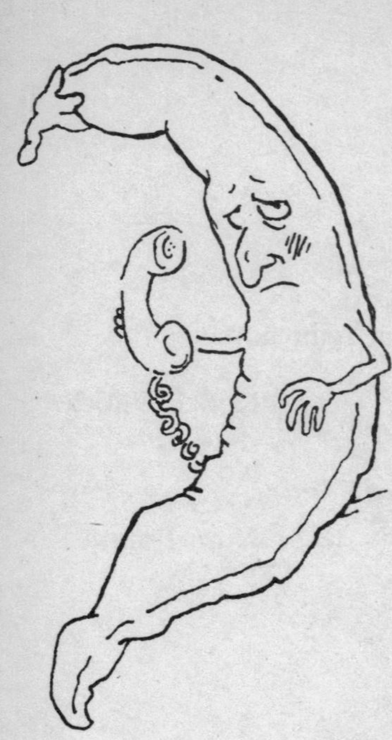

Knock, knock.
Who's there?
Bean.
Bean who?
Bean working very hard today.

Knock, knock.
Who's there?
Heaven.
Heaven who?
Heaven seen you for a long time.

Knock, knock.
Who's there?
Hope.
Hope who?
Hopefully that present is for me.

Knock, knock.
Who's there?
Bertha.
Bertha who?
Bertha-day greetings.

Knock, knock.
Who's there?
Dragon.
Dragon who?
Dragon your feet again.

Knock, knock.
Who's there?
Adlai.
Adlai who?
Adlai a bet on that.

Knock, knock.
Who's there?
Cows.
Cows who?
Cows go 'moo' not 'who'!

Knock, knock.
Who's there?
Tuna fish.
Tuna fish who?
You can tune a piano, but you can't tuna fish.

Knock, knock.
Who's there?
Consumption.
Consumption who?
Consumption be done about all these knock-knock jokes?

Knock, knock.
Who's there?
Argo.
Argo who?
Argo to Margate for my holidays.

Knock, knock.
Who's there?
Stanton.
Stanton who?
Stanton here in the cold is no fun.

Knock, knock.
Who's there?
Jaws.
Jaws who?
Jaws truly.

Knock, knock.
Who's there?
Tuna.
Tuna who?
Tuna your radio down, I'm trying to get some sleep.

Knock, knock.
Who's there?
Lettuce.
Lettuce who?
Lettuce try again tomorrow.

Knock, knock.
Who's there?
X.
X who?
X-tremely pleased to meet you.

Knock, knock.
Who's there?
Major.
Major who?
Major B. Hindsaw when you got caned.

Knock, knock.
Who's there?
Banana.
Banana who?
Banana split so ice creamed.

Knock, knock.
Who's there?
Annetta.
Annetta who?
Annetta joke like that and you're off this bus.

Knock, knock.
Who's there?
Haydn.
Haydn who?
Haydn seek is fun to play.

Knock, knock.
Who's there?
Farmer.
Farmer who?
Farmer birthday I'm going to have a new bike.

Knock, knock.
Who's there?
Osborne.
Osborne who?
Osborne today, it's my birthday.

Knock, knock.
Who's there?
Lock.
Lock who?
Lock who it is, after all this time!

Knock, knock.
Who's there?
Turnip.
Turnip who?
Turnip for work at nine or you're fired!

Knock, knock.
Who's there?
Nana.
Nana who?
Nana your business.

Knock, knock.
Who's there?
Rhoda.
Rhoda who?
Rhoda boat as fast as you can.

Knock, knock.
Who's there?
Amory.
Amory who?
Amory Christmas and a happy New Year to all our readers.

> Knock, knock.
> *Who's there?*
> Athena.
> *Athena who?*
> Athena reindeer landing on your roof.

> Knock, knock.
> *Who's there?*
> Gilda.
> *Gilda who?*
> Gilda fly that sat on the end of my nose.

Knock, knock.
Who's there?
Rhoda.
Rhoda who?
I Rhoda camel to school today and gave my teacher the
    hump.

Knock, knock.
Who's there?
Quacker.
Quacker who?
Quacker 'nother bad joke and I'm off!

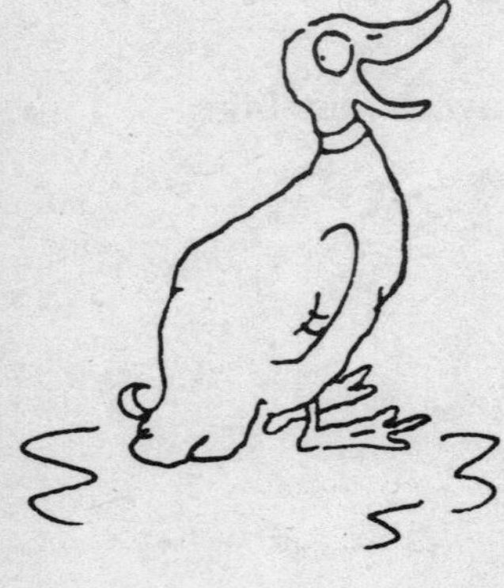

Knock, knock.
Who's there?
Marmite.
Marmite who?
Marmite but pa might not.

Knock, knock.
Who's there?
Datsun.
Datsun who?
Datsun old joke.

Knock, knock.
Who's there?
Deceit.
Deceit who?
Deceit of your trousers looks wet.

Knock, knock.
Who's there?
Noah.
Noah who?
Noah yes – which is it?

Knock, knock.
Who's there?
Ollie.
Ollie who?
Ollie time you do that I want to scream!

    Knock, knock.
    Who's there?
    Hominy.
    Hominy who?
    Hominy people live in this house?

        Knock, knock.
        Who's there?
        Ivan.
        Ivan who?
        Ivan idea you know who it is.

    Knock, knock.
    Who's there?
    Watson.
    Watson who?
    Watson the menu today?

Knock, knock.
Who's there?
Europe.
Europe who?
Europe early this morning.

    Knock, knock.
    Who's there?
    Meg.
    Meg who?
    Meg your bed before you get any breakfast.

    Knock, knock.
    Who's there?
    Aida.
    Aida who?
    Aida huge breakfast before going to school.

Knock, knock.
Who's there?
Howell.
Howell who?
Howell you have your toast, with marmalade or jam?

Knock, knock.
Who's there?
Egbert.
Egbert who?
Egbert no bacon.

    Knock, knock.
    Who's there?
    Boiler.
    Boiler who?
    Boiler egg for four minutes.

        Knock, knock.
        Who's there?
        Hammond.
        Hammond who?
        Hammond eggs.

Knock, knock.
Who's there?
Farmer.
Farmer who?
Farmer people here than there were last year.

Knock, knock.
Who's there?
Turnip.
Turnip who?
Turnip the heat, it's cold in here.

Knock, knock.
Who's there?
Man.
Man who?
Managed to get here then.

Knock, knock.
Who's there?
Kipper.
Kipper who?
Kipper hands to yourself.

Knock, knock.
Who's there?
York.
York who?
York coming over to our place.

Knock, knock.
Who's there?
Alison.
Alison who?
Alison to my radio in the mornings.

Knock, knock.
Who's there?
Doughnut.
Doughnut who?
Doughnut let anyone else in but me.

Knock, knock.
Who's there?
Fodder.
Fodder who?
Fodder and mother are taking me on holiday.

Knock, knock.
Who's there?
Darius.
Darius who?
Darius a lot I have to tell you.

Knock, knock.
Who's there?
Odessa.
Odessa who?
Odessa really funny face, man!

Knock, knock.
Who's there?
Zoo-keeper.
Zoo-keeper who?
Zoo-keeper way from me!

Knock, knock.
Who's there?
Cindy.
Cindy who?
Cindy next one in please.

Knock, knock.
Who's there?
Ether.
Ether who?
Ether bunny.

Knock, knock.
Who's there?
Plato.
Plato who?
Plato fish and chips please.

Knock, knock.
Who's there?
Dinah.
Dinah who?
Dinah is served.

Knock, knock.
Who's there?
Emma.
Emma who?
Emma pig when it comes to ice cream.

Knock, knock.
Who's there?
Roland.
Roland who?
Roland butter please.

Knock, knock.
Who's there?
Maida.
Maida who?
Maida cake 'cos you were coming.

Knock, knock.
Who's there?
Carmen.
Carmen who?
Carmen get it!

Knock, knock.
Who's there?
Genoa.
Genoa who?
Genoa new knock-knock joke?

Knock, knock.
Who's there?
Nose.
Nose who?
I nose plenty more knock-knock jokes, don't worry!

Moira See You, Moira Like You!

Knock, knock.
Who's there?
Moira.
Moira who?
Moira see you, Moira like you!

Knock, knock.
Who's there?
Cynthia.
Cynthia who?
Cynthia been gone I mith you very much.

Knock, knock.
Who's there?
Alfalfa.
Alfalfa who?
Alfalfa you if you fall for me.

Knock, knock.
Who's there?
Hollis.
Hollis who?
Hollis forgiven, come home.

Knock, knock.
Who's there?
Wah.
Wah who?
Well, you don't have to get excited just because I'm here!

Knock, knock.
Who's there?
Wicked.
Wicked who?
Wicked go for long walks together.

Knock, knock.
Who's there?
Eyesore.
Eyesore who?
Eyesore do like you!

Knock, knock.
Who's there?
Value.
Value who?
Value by my Valentine?

Knock, knock.
Who's there?
Butcher.
Butcher who?
Butcher arms around me.

Knock, knock.
Who's there?
Honeydew.
Honeydew who?
Honeydew you want to come out tonight?

Knock, knock.
Who's there?
Olive.
Olive who?
Olive you too, Honeybunch!

Knock, knock.
Who's there?
Guinevere.
Guinevere who?
Guinevere going to get together again?

Knock, knock.
Who's there?
Sauce.
Sauce who?
Sauce together, now she'll tell everyone.

Knock, knock.
Who's there?
Felix.
Felix who?
Felix Ited, about meeting you.

Knock, knock.
Who's there?
Anthem.
Anthem who?
U. Anthem devil you.

Knock, knock.
Who's there?
Alice.
Alice who?
Alice forgiven, please come home.

Knock, knock.
Who's there?
Pyjamas.
Pyjamas who?
Pyjamas 'round me honey, hold me tight.

Knock, knock.
Who's there?
Gwen.
Gwen who?
Gwen will I see you again?

Knock, knock.
Who's there?
Sherry.
Sherry who?
Sherry dance?

Knock, knock.
Who's there?
Murray.
Murray who?
Murray me! Not likely!

Knock, knock.
Who's there?
Oliver.
Oliver who?
Oliver, but she doesn't love me.

Knock, knock.
Who's there?
Congo.
Congo who?
Congo on meeting like this.

Knock, knock.
Who's there?
Myth.
Myth who?
Myth you too.

Yukon Say That Again

Buddha This Slice of Bread for Me
or
Wise Sayings from the East

Knock, knock.
Who's there?
Buddha.
Buddha who?
Buddha this slice of bread for me.

Knock, knock.
Who's there?
Yulla.
Yulla who?
Yulla catch more flies with honey than vinegar.

    Knock, knock.
    Who's there?
    Zeke.
    Zeke who?
    Zeke and ye shall find.

Knock, knock.
Who's there?
Pudding.
Pudding who?
Pudding on your shoes before your trousers is a bad idea.

Knock, knock.
Who's there?
Tish.
Tish who?
Tish who is good for blowing your nose.

    Knock, knock.
    Who's there?
    Carlotta.
    Carlotta who?
    Carlotta trouble when it breaks down.

Knock, knock.
Who's there?
Cargo.
Cargo who?
Cargo better if you fill it with petrol first.

Knock, knock.
Who's there?
Your pencil.
Your pencil who?
Your pencil fall down if you don't wear a belt or suspenders.

Knock, knock.
Who's there?
Fiddlestick.
Fiddlestick who?
Fiddlestick out of the bottom of the bed if you're too tall.

     Knock, knock.
     Who's there?
     Seymour.
     Seymour who?
     Seymour if you look out of the window.

          Knock, knock.
          Who's there?
          Lionel.
          Lionel who?
          Lionel roar if you don't feed him.

Knock, knock.
Who's there?
Lucy.
Lucy who?
Lucy Lastic can be embarrassing.

     Knock, knock.
     Who's there?
     Luke.
     Luke who?
     Luke before you leap.

     Knock, knock.
     Who's there?
     Constance Norah.
     Constance Norah who?
     Constance Norahs make it difficult to sleep.

Knock, knock.
Who's there?
Howard.
Howard who?
Howard the ground is when you slip on a banana skin.

     Knock, knock.
     Who's there?
     Wanda.
     Wanda who?
     Wanda off and you'll get lost.

     Knock, knock.
     Who's there?
     Cattle.
     Cattle who?
     Cattle always purr when you stroke her.

Knock, knock.
Who's there?
Lucifer.
Lucifer who?
Lucifer coat and you'll be cold.

Knock, knock.
Who's there?
Tuna.
Tuna who?
Tuna violin and it will sound better.

Familiar Phrases

Knock, knock.
Who's there?
Yukon.
Yukon who?
Yukon say that again.

Knock, knock.
Who's there?
Ellie.
Ellie who?
Ellie Phants never forget.

Knock, knock.
Who's there?
Denver.
Denver who?
Denver the good old days.

Knock, knock.
Who's there?
Percy.
Percy who?
Percy Vere and you'll succeed.

Knock, knock.
Who's there?
Spook.
Spook who?
Spook only when you are spoken to.

Knock, knock.
Who's there?
Wannetta.
Wannetta who?
Wannetta time, please!

Knock, knock.
Who's there?
Schatzi.
Schatzi who?
Schatzi way to do it.

Knock, knock.
Who's there?
John.
John who?
John the Navy and see the world.

Knock, knock.
Who's there?
Sizzle.
Sizzle who?
Sizzle hurt me more than it will you.

Knock, knock.
Who's there?
Omega.
Omega who?
Omega best man win.

Knock, knock.
Who's there?
Teddy.
Teddy who?
Teddy is the beginning of the rest of your life.

Knock, knock.
Who's there?
Emile.
Emile who?
Emile fit for a king.

Knock, knock.
Who's there?
Toucan.
Toucan who?
Toucan live as cheaply as one.

Knock, knock.
Who's there?
Yukon.
Yukon who?
Yukon fool some of the people some of the time . . .

Knock, knock.
Who's there?
Tex.
Tex who?
Tex two to tango.

Knock, knock.
Who's there?
Willoughby.
Willoughby who?
Willoughby a monkey's uncle!

Knock, knock.
Who's there?
Arnold.
Arnold who?
Arnold friend of yours is a friend of mine.

Knock, knock.
Who's there?
Zizi.
Zizi who?
Zizi when you know how.

Knock, knock.
Who's there?
Dawn.
Dawn who?
Dawn do anything I wouldn't do.

Knock, knock.
Who's there?
Hair.
Hair who?
Hair today and gone tomorrow.

Knock, knock.
Who's there?
Sharon.
Sharon who?
Sharon share alike.

Knock, knock.
Who's there?
Cigarette.
Cigarette who?
Cigarette life if you don't weaken.

Knock, knock.
Who's there?
Mortimer.
Mortimer who?
Mortimer than meets the eye.

Knock, knock.
Who's there?
Lilac.
Lilac who?
Lilac a trooper.

Knock, knock.
Who's there?
Watusi.
Watusi who?
Watusi is what you get!

Knock, knock.
Who's there?
Eustace.
Eustace who?
Come Eustace you are.

Knock, knock.
Who's there?
Sofa.
Sofa who?
Sofa so good.

Knock, knock.
Who's there?
Radio.
Radio who?
Radio not, here I come.

Knock, knock.
Who's there?
Don.
Don who?
Don just stand there, say something.

Clichés

Knock, knock.
Who's there?
Holmes.
Holmes who?
Holmes is where the heart is.

Knock, knock.
Who's there?
Roland.
Roland who?
Roland stone gathers no moss.

Knock, knock.
Who's there?
Manny.
Manny who?
Manny are called, but few are chosen.

    Knock, knock.
    Who's there?
    Burton.
    Burton who?
    Burton the hand is worth two in the bush.

        Knock, knock.
        Who's there?
        Dotty.
        Dotty who?
        Dotty way the cookie crumbles.

Knock, knock.
Who's there?
Yukon.
Yukon who?
Yukon lead a horse to water, but you can't make it drink.

    Knock, knock.
    Who's there?
    Oily.
    Oily who?
    The oily bird catches the worm.

        Knock, knock.
        Who's there?
        Opera.
        Opera who?
        Opera-tunity only knocks once

Knock, knock.
Who's there?
Tibet.
Tibet who?
Early Tibet, early to rise.

    Knock, knock.
    Who's there?
    Mary.
    Mary who?
    Mary in haste, repent at leisure.

Literary Lines

Knock, knock.
Who's there?
Rita.
Rita who?
Rita good book, you might learn something.

Knock, knock.
Who's there?
Gnu.
Gnu who?
Gnu lamps for old!

Knock, knock.
Who's there?
Eve.
Eve who?
Eve ho my hearties!

Knock, knock.
Who's there?
Hoffman.
Hoffman who?
I'll Hoffman I'll puff, and I'll blow your house down.

Knock, knock.
Who's there?
Saul.
Saul who?
Saul the king's horses, and saul the king's men.

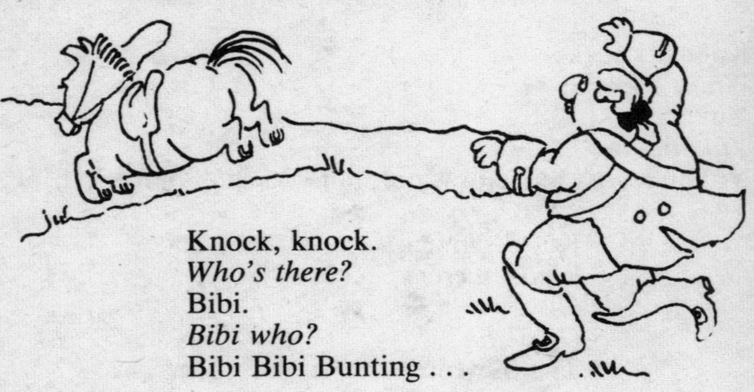

Knock, knock.
Who's there?
Bibi.
Bibi who?
Bibi Bibi Bunting . . .

Knock, knock.
Who's there?
Thumb.
Thumb who?
Thumb like it hot, thumb like it cold . . .

Knock, knock.
Who's there?
Franz.
Franz who?
Franz, Romans, countrymen, lend me your ears.

Knock, knock.
Who's there?
Ella Mann.
Ella Mann who?
Ella Mann-Tree, my dear Watson.

Knock, knock.
Who's there?
Ooze.
Ooze who?
Ooze been sleeping in my bed?

Knock, knock.
Who's there?
Toby.
Toby who?
Toby or not to be.

Knock, knock.
Who's there?
Thaddeus.
Thaddeus who?
Thaddeus the question.

In Person

A chance for you to try out some impersonations!

Knock, knock.
Who's there?
Elephant.
Elephant who?
Elephant A. Sizes about being a Hollywood star.

Mae West

Knock, knock.
Who's there?
Welcome.
Welcome who?
Welcome up and see me sometime.

Knock, knock.
Who's there?
Collier.
Collier who?
Collier self a man do you!

Knock, knock.
Who's there?
Warrior.
Warrior who?
Warrior been all my life?

Greta Garbo

Knock, knock.
Who's there?
Yvonne.
Yvonne who?
Yvonne to be alone.

W. C. Fields

Knock, knock.
Who's there?
Melita.
Melita who?
Melita chickadee.

Bruce Forsyth

Knock, knock.
Who's there?
Noise.
Noise who?
Noise to see yer.

Bugs Bunny

Knock, knock.
Who's there?
Yacht.
Yacht who?
Yacht's up, Doc?

Humphrey Bogart

Knock, knock.
Who's there?
Ears.
Ears who?
Ears looking at you, kid.

Graucho Marx

Knock, knock.
Who's there?
Ella.
Ella who?
Ella Vator. Doesn't that give you a lift?

Knock, knock.
Who's there?
Little old lady.
Little old lady who?
My! You're good a yodelling?

Knock, knock.
Who's there?
Beets.
Beets who?
Beets me, but I just forgot the joke

Knock, knock.
Who's there?
Ice cream.
Ice cream who?
Ice cream and scream and scream until I'm sick.

Knock, knock.
Who's there?
Cellar.
Cellar who?
Cellar. No, I think she can be repaired.

Knock, knock.
Who's there?
Odel-lay-he.
Odel-lay-he who?
Didn't know you could yodel.

Knock, knock.
Who's there?
Juno.
Juno who?
Of course I do!

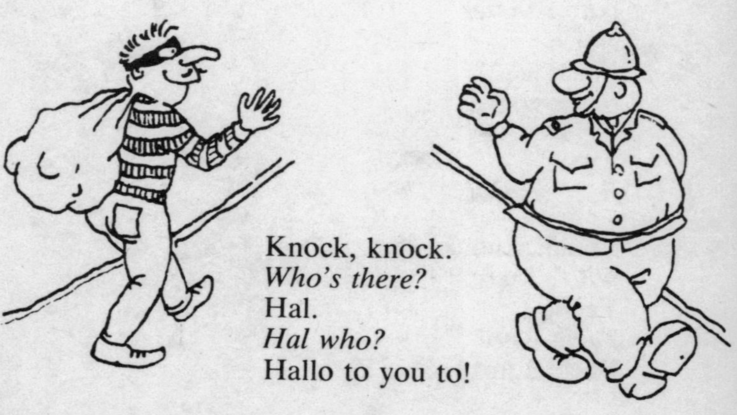

Knock, knock.
Who's there?
Hal.
Hal who?
Hallo to you to!

Knock, knock.
Who's there?
Ike.
Ike who?
Ike Ent stop laughing.

> Knock, knock.
> *Who's there?*
> Statue.
> *Statue who?*
> Statue? This is me.

> Knock, knock.
> *Who's there?*
> Alfred.
> *Alfred who?*
> Alfred the needle if you sew.

Knock, knock.
Who's there?
Worzel.
Worzel who?
It's upstairs – first on the left.

> Knock, knock.
> *Who's there?*
> Tilly.
> *Tilly who?*
> What are you then – a fox-hunter?

> Knock, knock.
> *Who's there?*
> Yah.
> *Yah who?*
> Ride 'em cowboy!

Knock, knock.
Who's there?
Cook.
Cook who?
That's the first I've heard this year.

> Knock, knock.
> *Who's there?*
> Toodle.
> *Toodle who?*
> Bye, bye!

Sarah Doctor in the House?

Knock, knock.
Who's there?
Sarah.
Sarah who?
Sarah doctor in the house?

Knock, knock.
Who's there?
Ivan.
Ivan who?
Ivan infectious disease.
Slam!

Knock, knock.
Who's there?
Aileen.
Aileen who?
Aileen Dover and fell down.

Knock, knock.
Who's there?
Artichoke.
Artichoke who?
Artichoke when he swallowed his yo-yo.

Knock, knock.
Who's there?
Atch.
Atch who?
Nasty cold you've got.

Knock, knock.
Who's there?
Colin.
Colin who?
Colin the doctor, I'm not well

Knock, knock.
Who's there?
Elke.
Elke who?
Elke Seltzer . . . plop, plop, fizz.

Knock, knock.
Who's there?
Aida.
Aida who?
Aida lot of green apples, now I feel sick.

Knock, knock.
Who's there?
Arch.
Arch who?
Sounds like you got the 'flu.

Knock, knock.
Who's there?
Jessica.
Jessica who?
Jessica than I thought. I'll get a doctor.

Knock, knock.
Who's there?
Atomic.
Atomic who?
Atomic ache.

Knock, knock.
Who's there?
Agatha.
Agatha who?
Agatha headache. Got an aspirin?

Knock, knock.
Who's there?
Money.
Money who?
Money is stiff since I knocked it on the table leg.

Knock, knock.
Who's there?
Stan.
Stan who?
Stan back, I'm going to sneeze.

Knock, knock.
Who's there?
Dai.
Dai who?
Dai Larfin.

Knock, knock.
Who's there?
Mummy.
Mummy who?
Mummeasles are better so can I come in?

Knock, knock.
Who's there?
Santa.
Santa who?
Santa forward in our team was ill today.

Knock, knock.
Who's there?
Major.
Major who?
Major headache, that noise.

Knock, knock.
Who's there?
Lee.
Lee who?
Lee me alone! I've got a headache.

Knock, knock.
Who's there?
Illegal.
Illegal who?
Illegals stay in the nest until they feel better.

Knock, knock.
Who's there?
Paul Lee.
Paul Lee who?
Feeling Paul Lee, so stayed in bed.

Knock, knock.
Who's there?
Bless.
Bless who?
I didn't sneeze!

Knock, knock.
Who's there?
Abbey.
Abbey who?
Abbey stung me on the nose.

Knock, knock.
Who's there?
Hatch.
Hatch who?
God Bless you.

Knock, knock.
Who's there?
Myope.
Myope who?
Myope is that you get well soon.

World Affairs

Knock, knock.
Who's there?
Europe.
Europe who?
Europe to no good.

Knock, knock.
Who's there?
Venice.
Venice who?
Venice your mother coming home?

Knock, knock.
Who's there?
Sicily.
Sicily who?
Sicily question to ask.

Knock, knock.
Who's there?
Lisa.
Lisa who?
Lisa you can do is let me in.

Knock, knock.
Who's there?
Viola.
Viola who?
Viola sudden you don't want me to come in?

Knock, knock.
Who's there?
Yolanda.
Yolanda who?
Yolanda me some money?

Knock, knock.
Who's there?
Bella.
Bella who?
Bella not-a work so I knock-a on-a de door!

Knock, knock.
Who's there?
Vanessa.
Vanessa who?
Vanessa you going to grow up?

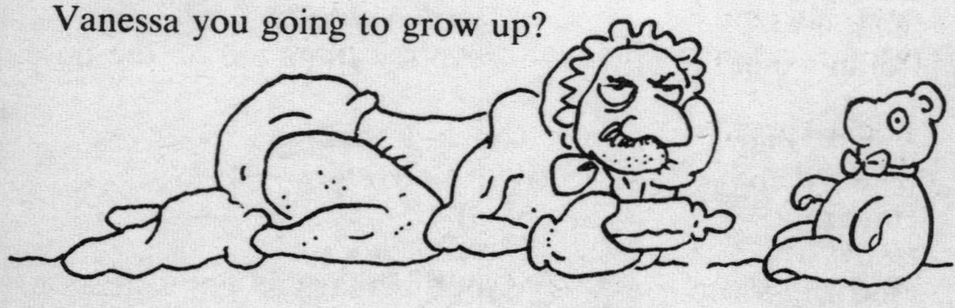

Knock, knock.
Who's there?
Isiah.
Isiah who?
Isiah nothing till you open the door.

Knock, knock.
Who's there?
Hanover.
Hanover who?
Hanover the money!

Knock, knock.
Who's there?
Harvey.
Harvey who?
Harvey gonna play this game forever.

Knock, knock.
Who's there?
Avon.
Avon who?
Avon who to come and open zis door.

Knock, knock.
Who's there?
Mitzi.
Mitzi who?
Mitzi door shut you'll never find out.

Knock, knock.
Who's there?
Weavish.
Weavish who?
Weavish you a merry Christmas and a happy New Year.

Knock, knock.
Who's there?
Sophie.
Sophie who?
Sophie come to the end of the lesson.

Knock, knock.
Who's there?
Weevil.
Weevil who?
Weevil only be staying a minute.

Knock, knock.
Who's there?
Veal chop.
Veal chop who?
Veal chop around and see what bargains vee can pick up.

Knock, knock.
Who's there?
Dwayne.
Dwayne who?
Dwayne in Spain falls mainly on the plain.

Knock, knock.
Who's there?
Valencia.
Valencia who?
Valencia pound when will I get it back?

Knock, knock.
Who's there?
Marcella.
Marcella who?
Marcella's full of water.

Knock, knock.
Who's there?
Senor.
Senor who?
Senor mother out and let me in.

Knock, knock.
Who's there?
Juanita.
Juanita who?
Juanita 'nother hot dog?

Knock, knock.
Who's there?
Don Giovanni.
Don Giovanni who?
Don Giovanni talk to me anymore?

Knock, knock.
Who's there?
Don Juan.
Don Juan who?
Don Juan to go out today?

Knock, knock.
Who's there?
Don Juan.
Don Juan who?
Don Juan to stay out here forever?

Knock, knock.
Who's there?
Signor.
Signor who?
Signor light on, so I knocked.

Knock, knock.
Who's there?
Summertime.
Summertime who?
Summertime you can be a big pest.

Knock, knock.
Who's there?
Francis.
Francis who?
Francis the other side of the channel.

Knock, knock.
Who's there?
Francis.
Francis who?
Francis where people speak French.

Knock, knock.
Who's there?
Monkey.
Monkey who?
Monkey won't fit, that's why I can't get in.

Knock, knock.
Who's there?
Oslo.
Oslo who?
Oslo down. What's the hurry?

Knock, knock.
Who's there?
Ireland.
Ireland who?
Ireland you some money if you promise to pay me back.

Knock, knock.
Who's there?
Irish.
Irish who?
Irish you would come out and play with me.

Knock, knock.
Who's there?
Diesel.
Diesel who?
Diesel be your bags on the step I suppose?

Knock, knock.
Who's there?
Otis.
Otis who?
Otis a wonderful day for a walk in the park.

Knock, knock.
Who's there?
Ottawa.
Ottawa who?
Ottawa know you're telling the truth?

Knock, knock.
Who's there?
Havana.
Havana who?
Havana wonderful time, wish you were here.

Knock, knock.
Who's there?
Cantaloupe.
Cantaloupe who?
Cantaloupe with you tonight.

Knock, knock.
Who's there?
Egypt.
Egypt who?
Egypt a bit off my best china plate.

Knock, knock.
Who's there?
Solly.
Solly who?
Solly you been troubled, me makee mistakee.

Knock, knock.
Who's there?
Abyssinia.
Abyssinia who?
Abyssinia when I get back.

Knock, knock.
Who's there?
Quebec.
Quebec who?
Quebec to the back of the queue.

Knock, knock.
Who's there?
Alaska.
Alaska who?
Alaska my mummy.

Knock, knock.
Who's there?
Russian.
Russian who?
Russian about makes me tired.

Knock, knock.
Who's there?
Armenia.
Armenia who?
Armenia every word I say.

Knock, knock.
Who's there?
Indonesia.
Indonesia who?
I look at you and I get weak Indonesia.

Knock, knock.
Who's there?
Asia.
Asia who?
Asia going to invite me in?

Knock, knock.
Who's there?
Iran.
Iran who?
Iran away when you answered before.

Knock, knock.
Who's there?
India.
India who?
India good old summertime.

Knock, knock.
Who's there?
Bolivia.
Bolivia who?
Bolivia me, I know what I'm talking about.

Knock, knock.
Who's there?
Jamaica.
Jamaica who?
Jamaica mistake?

Knock, knock.
Who's there?
Huron.
Huron who?
Huron time for once.

Knock, knock.
Who's there?
Ann.
Ann who?
Ann Tarctic.

Knock, knock.
Who's there?
Amazon.
Amazon who?
Amazon of a bishop. What's your father do?

Knock, knock.
Who's there?
Amana.
Amana who?
Amana very bad mood.

Tarzan Stripes Forever

Knock, knock.
Who's there?
Tarzan.
Tarzan who?
Tarzan Stripes Forever.

Knock, knock.
Who's there?
Llama.
Llama who?
Llama Yankee Doodle Dandy.

Knock, knock.
Who's there?
Cereal.
Cereal who?
Cereal pleasure to meet you.

Knock, knock.
Who's there?
Sherwood.
Sherwood who?
Sherwood like to meet you.

Knock, knock.
Who's there?
Alpaca.
Alpaca who?
Alpaca picnic lunch.

Knock, knock.
Who's there?
Arizona.
Arizona who?
Arizona room for one of us.

Knock, knock.
Who's there?
Ida.
Ida who?
It's not Ida who, it's Idaho.

Knock, knock.
Who's there?
Kentucky.
Kentucky who?
Kentucky come out to play?

Knock, knock.
Who's there?
Louisiana.
Louisiana who?
Louisiana boy-friend broke up.

Knock, knock.
Who's there?
Minneapolis.
Minneapolis who?
Minneapolis a day keeps the doctor away.

Knock, knock.
Who's there?
Zippy.
Zippy who?
Mrs. Zippy.

Knock, knock.
Who's there?
Nantucket.
Nantucket who?
Nantucket, but she'll have to give it back.

Knock, knock.
Who's there?
Nevada.
Nevada who?
Nevada saw you look worse, you should be in bed.

Knock, knock.
Who's there?
Tennessee.
Tennessee who?
Tennessee you tonight?

Knock, knock.
Who's there?
Tucson.
Tucson who?
Tucson an' two daughters are enough kids.

Knock, knock.
Who's there?
Utah.
Utah who?
Utah sight, utah mind.

Knock, knock.
Who's there?
Utah.
Utah who?
Utah the road and I'll mend the fence.

Knock, knock.
Who's there?
Yukon.
Yukon who?
Yukon go away and come back at a reasonable time.

Knock, knock.
Who's there?
Yukon.
Yukon who?
Yukon say that again.
Ok, I will. Knock, knock.
Who's there?
Yukon.
(Repeat over and over.)

I Didn't Come Here to be Insulted!

Knock, knock.
Who's there?
Cook.
Cook who?
Cuckoo yourself! I didn't come here to be insulted!

Knock, knock.
Who's there?
Al.
Al who?
Al go home if you're not nice to me.

Knock, knock.
Who's there?
Gopher.
Gopher who?
Gopher a long walk off a short pier.

Knock, knock.
Who's there?
Dummy.
Dummy who?
Dummy a favour and get lost.

Knock, knock.
Who's there?
Sir.
Sir who?
Sir View right!

Knock, knock.
Who's there?
Frank.
Frank who?
Frank Lee, I don't care.

Knock, knock.
Who's there?
Hugo.
Hugo who?
Hugo jump in the lake.

Knock, knock.
Who's there?
Urchin.
Urchin who?
Urchin is pointed!

Knock, knock.
Who's there?
Howard.
Howard who?
Howard you like a punch on the nose?

Knock, knock.
Who's there?
Ogre.
Ogre who?
Ogre take a running
                    jump.

Knock, knock.
Who's there?
Cash.
Cash who?
I didn't realize you were some kind of nut.

Knock, knock.
Who's there?
Pecan.
Pecan who?
Pecan somebody your own size.

Knock, knock.
Who's there?
Watson.
Watson who?
Watson your head?

Knock, knock.
Who's there?
Poker.
Poker who?
Poker and see if she's awake.

Knock, knock.
Who's there?
Danielle.
Danielle who?
Danielle at me, it's not my fault.

Knock, knock.
Who's there?
Orson.
Orson who?
Stop Orson around and let me in.

Knock, knock.
Who's there?
Closure.
Closure who?
Closure mouth, I'm talking.

Knock, knock.
Who's there?
Scott.
Scott who?
Scott nothing to do with you.

Knock, knock.
Who's there?
Water-skier.
Water-skier who?
Water-skier Dof? It won't hurt you.

Knock, knock.
Who's there?
Enid.
Enid who?
Enid spanking for being so rude.

Knock, knock.
Who's there?
Boo.
Boo who?
No need to cry – it's only a joke.

Knock, knock.
Who's there?
William.
William who?
William mind your own business!

Knock, knock.
Who's there?
Ida.
Ida who?
Ida face, she's so ugly!

Knock, knock.
Who's there?
Hawaii.
Hawaii who?
Fine, until you showed up.

Knock, knock.
Who's there?
Water.
Water who?
Water be ashamed of yourself!

Knock, knock.
Who's there?
Thayer.
Thayer who?
Thayer thorry.

Knock, knock.
Who's there?
Tomorr.
Tomorr who?
Got a speech impediment have you?

Knock, knock.
Who's there?
Acid.
Acid who?
Acid-own and be quiet!

Knock, knock.
Who's there?
Fatso.
Fatso who?
Fatso matter with you?

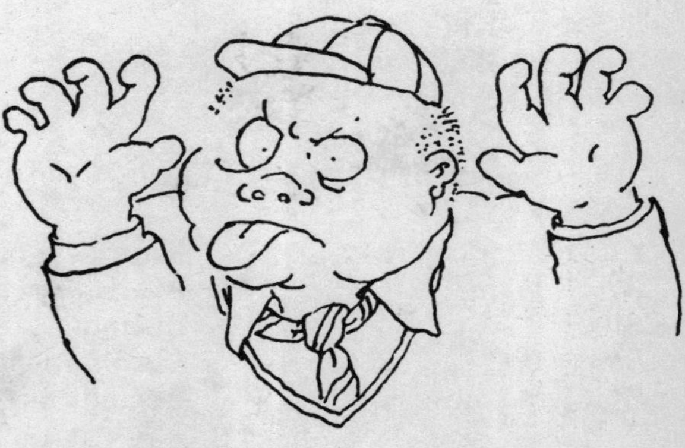

More Knock–Knocks

Knock, knock.
Who's there?
Ears.
Ears who?
Ears some more knock-knock jokes for you.

Knock, knock.
Who's there?
Hosanna.
Hosanna who?
Hosanna Claus gets down the chimney I'll never know.

Knock, knock.
Who's there?
Ketchup.
Ketchup who?
Ketchup with me and I'll tell you.

Knock, knock.
Who's there?
Mary.
Mary who?
Mary Christmas.

Knock, knock.
Who's there?
Rabbit.
Rabbit who?
Rabbit up nicely, it's a present.

Knock, knock.
Who's there?
Noel.
Noel who?
Noel E. Phant is going to poke his trunk in my business.

Knock, knock.
Who's there?
Dunce.
Dunce who?
Dunce A. another word.

Knock, knock.
Who's there?
Kojak.
Kojak who?
Kojak up the car, I've got a flat tyre.

Knock, knock.
Who's there?
Spider.
Spider who?
Spider when she thought I wasn't looking.

Knock, knock.
Who's there?
Blue
Blue who?
Blue your nose.

Knock, knock.
Who's there?
Lucinda.
Lucinda who?
Lucinda sky with diamonds.

Knock, knock.
Who's there?
Hardy.
Hardy who?
Hardy hi!

Knock, knock.
Who's there?
Spook.
Spook who?
Spook-etti.

Knock, knock.
Who's there?
Socket.
Socket who?
Socket to me.

Knock, knock.
Who's there?
Pasture.
Pasture who?
Pasture your bedtime isn't it?

Knock, knock.
Who's there?
Xavier.
Xavier who?
Xavier money for a rainy day.

Knock, knock.
Who's there?
Ivan.
Ivan who?
It's not Ivan who, it's Ivanhoe.

Knock, knock.
Who's there?
Whistle.
Whistle who?
Whistle be going home soon.

Knock, knock.
Who's there?
Arthur.
Arthur who?
Arthur any biscuits left?

Knock, knock.
Who's there?
Juno.
Juno who?
Juno what time it is?

Knock, knock.
Who's there?
Avenue.
Avenue who?
Avenue heard the good news?

Knock, knock.
Who's there?
Minerva.
Minerva who?
Minerva Zereckt from all these questions.

Knock, knock.
Who's there?
Watson.
Watson who?
What's on television tonight?

Knock, knock.
Who's there?
July.
July who?
July to me about stealing my pencil?

Knock, knock.
Who's there?
Walrus.
Walrus who?
Why do you walrus ask that silly question?

Knock, knock.
Who's there?
Waiter.
Waiter who?
Waiter minute while I tie my shoelaces up.

Knock, knock.
Who's there?
Sacha.
Sacha who?
Sacha lot of questions.

Knock, knock.
Who's there?
Moose.
Moose who?
Moose you be so nosey?

Knock, knock.
Who's there?
Alex.
Alex who?
Alex the questions, if you don't mind.

Knock, knock.
Who's there?
Noah.
Noah who?
Noah good place to eat?

Knock, knock.
Who's there?
Canoe.
Canoe who?
Canoe come out to play?

Knock, knock.
Who's there?
I don't know.
I don't know who?
I told you I don't know. Why don't you believe me?

Knock, knock.
Who's there?
Ivan.
Ivan who?
Ivanhoe, by Sir Walter Scott.

Knock, knock.
Who's there?
Thatcher.
Thatcher who?
Thatcher could get away with it.

Knock, knock.
Who's there?
Midas.
Midas who?
Midas well relax. I'm not going anywhere.

Knock, knock.
Who's there?
Earl.
Earl who?
Earl be glad to get to bed, I'm tired.

Knock, knock.
Who's there?
Jaguar.
Jaguar who?
Jaguar nimble, Jaguar quick . . .

Knock, knock.
Who's there?
Teacher.
Teacher who?
Teacher to go knocking on my door in the middle of
  the night.

Knock, knock.
Who's there?
Minnie.
Minnie who?
No, not Minniewho – Minniehaha.

Knock, knock.
Who's there?
Wheel barrow.
Wheel barrow who?
Wheel barrow some money and go on a trip.

Knock, knock.
Who's there?
Dewey.
Dewey who?
Dewey have to listen to anymore knock-knock jokes?

Knock, knock.
Who's there?
Owl.
Owl who?
Owl aboard the Skylark!

Knock, knock.
Who's there?
Hubbard.
Hubbard who?
Hubbard can sing louder than my bird.

Knock, knock.
Who's there?
Aunt Lou.
Aunt Lou who?
Aunt Lou tired of knocking on this door?

Knock, knock.
Who's there?
Harmony.
Harmony who?
Harmony knock-knock jokes do you expect me to know?

Knock, knock.
Who's there?
Handsome.
Handsome who?
Handsome sweets through the door and I'll tell you more.

Knock, knock.
Who's there?
Atlas.
Atlas who?
Atlas it's Friday, the week-end's here.

Knock, knock.
Who's there?
Sofa.
Sofa who?
Sofa we haven't made any mistakes.

Knock, knock.
Who's there?
Butcher.
Butcher who?
Butcher money where your mouth is.

Knock, knock.
Who's there?
Lion.
Lion who?
Lion on your doorstep, open up!

Knock, knock.
Who's there?
Kent.
Kent who?
Kent you guess who it is?

Knock, knock.
Who's there?
Thumping.
Thumping who?
Thumping green and slimey is climbing up your neck.

Knock, knock.
Who's there?
Sid.
Sid who?
Sid down and I'll make you a nice cup of tea.

Knock, knock.
Who's there?
Snow.
Snow who?
Snow good asking me – I don't know.

Knock, knock.
Who's there?
Pollyanna.
Pollyanna who?
Pollyanna bad kid when you get to know her.

Knock, knock.
Who's there?
Juicy.
Juicy who?
Juicy that rude sign on the door?

Knock, knock.
Who's there?
Halibut.
Halibut who?
Halibut letting me in on the secret?

Knock, knock.
Who's there?
Weirdo.
Weirdo who?
Weirdo you think you're going?

Knock, knock.
Who's there?
Voodoo.
Voodoo who?
Voodoo you think you are, Superman?

Knock, knock.
Who's there?
Dustin Hoffman.
Dustin Hoffman who?
Dustin Hoffman welcome mat for you.

Knock, knock.
Who's there?
Lloyd.
Lloyd who?
He Lloyd to me, he said it was Wednesday and it's only
    Tuesday!

Knock, knock.
Who's there?
Derek.
Derek who?
Derek of the Hesperus is a famous poem by Longfellow.

Knock, knock.
Who's there?
Wilson.
Wilson who?
Wilson be there.

      Knock, knock.
      Who's there?
      Conan.
      Conan who?
      Conan wafers go well with ice cream.

Knock, knock.
Who's there?
Old King Cole.
Old King Cole who?
Old King Cole, so turn the heat up.

      Knock, knock.
      Who's there?
      Four eggs.
      Four eggs who?
      Four eggs ample.

Knock, knock.
Who's there?
Gopher.
Gopher who?
Gopher your gun, Sheriff.

         Knock, knock.
         Who's there?
         Tina.
         Tina who?
         Pilchards.

               Knock, knock.
               Who's there?
               Ada.
               Ada who?
               First Ada Kit.

Knock, knock.
Who's there?
Eskimo.
Eskimo who?
Eskimo questions, I'll tell you no lies.

Knock, knock.
Who's there?
Harold.
Harold who?
Harold are you?

Knock, knock.
Who's there?
Warner.
Warner who?
Warner you coming out to play?

Knock, knock.
Who's there?
Dino.
Dino who?
Dino the answer.

Knock, knock.
Who's there?
Grannie. Knock, knock.
Who's there?
Grannie. Knock, knock.
Who's there?
Grannie. Knock, knock.
Who's there?
Grannie. Knock, knock.
Who's there?
Aunt.
Aunt who?
Aunt you glad Grannie's gone?

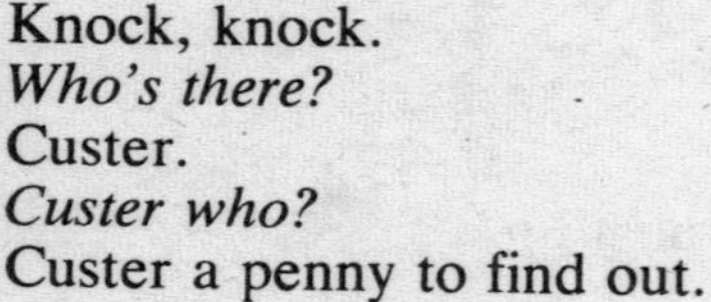

Knock, knock.
Who's there?
Custer.
Custer who?
Custer a penny to find out.

Knock, knock.
Who's there?
Dennis.
Dennis who?
Dennis says I need a filling.

Knock, knock.
Who's there?
Midas.
Midas who?
Midas well have stayed at home for all you care.

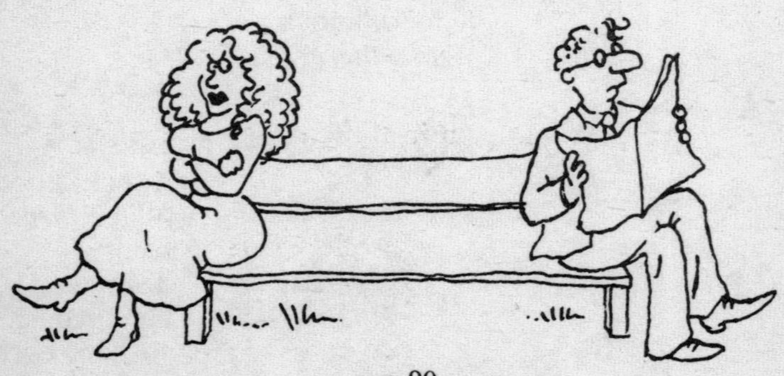

Knock, knock.
Who's there?
Jupiter.
Jupiter who?
Jupiter fly in my soup?

    Knock, knock.
    Who's there?
    Arthur.
    Arthur who?
    Arthur any cats in your house?

        Knock, knock.
        Who's there?
        Stu.
        Stu who?
        Stu late to ask questions.

Knock, knock.
Who's there?
Dozen.
Dozen who?
Dozen anybody want to play with me?

    Knock, knock.
    Who's there?
    Howie.
    Howie who?
    I'm okay. How are you?

Knock, knock.
Who's there?
Candy.
Candy who?
Candy cow jump over the moon?

        Knock, knock.
        Who's there?
        Watson.
        Watson who?
        Watson your mind?

    Knock, knock.
    Who's there?
    Howie.
    Howie who?
    Howie Dewin then?

Knock, knock.
Who's there?
Zany.
Zany who?
Zany body here seen Kelly?

    Knock, knock.
    Who's there?
    Athene.
    Athene who?
    Athene you in the butchers, haven't I?

        Knock, knock.
        Who's there?
        Ooze.
        Ooze who?
        Ooze in charge around here?

Knock, knock.
Who's there?
Owl.
Owl who?
Owl I can say is 'knock-knock'.

    Knock, knock.
    Who's there?
    Jess.
    Jess who?
    Jess one of those things, I suppose.

        Knock, knock.
        Who's there?
        Juicy.
        Juicy who?
        Juicy what I just saw?

            Knock, knock.
            Who's there?
            Scold.
            Scold who?
            Scold enough for snow.

Knock, knock.
Who's there?
Linda.
Linda who?
Linda hand, I can't be expected to do it all by myself!

Knock, knock.
Who's there?
Caesar.
Caesar who?
Caesar quickly before she gets away.

Knock, knock.
Who's there?
Ida.
Ida who?
Ida terrible time getting here.

Knock, knock.
Who's there?
Chin.
Chin who?
Chin up. I'm not going to tell you any more knock-knocks.

Knock, knock.
Who's there?
Al.
Al who?
Al lied.

        Knock, knock.
        Who's there?
        Torch.
        Torch who?
        Torch you would never ask.

            Knock, knock.
            Who's there?
            Ozzie.
            Ozzie who?
            Ozzie you later, ok?

Knock, knock.
Who's there?
Turnip.
Turnip who?
Turnip this little lane, that's where I live.

Knock, knock.
Who's there?
Wafer.
Wafer who?
Wafer a long time, but here I am again.

Knock, knock.
Who's there?
Cyril.
Cyril who?
Cyril thing – no imitations here.

Knock, knock.
Who's there?
Scold.
Scold who?
Scold enough to go ice-skating, isn't it.

Knock, knock.
Who's there?
Tamara.
Tamara who?
Tamara is Tuesday; today is Monday.

Knock, knock.
Who's there?
Mine.
Mine who?
Mine u hat just blew away.

Knock, knock.
Who's there?
Ivory.
Ivory who?
Ivory strong; how strong are you?

Knock, knock.
Who's there?
Maor.
Major who?
Major answer the knock-knock joke!

Knock, knock.
Who's there?
Lee King.
Lee King who?
Lee King Bucket.

Knock, knock.
Who's there?
Victor.
Victor who?
Victor his trousers getting here.

Knock, knock.
Who's there?
Tank.
Tank who?
My pleasure.

Knock, knock.
Who's there?
Nurse.
Nurse who?
Nurse sense in talking to you.

Knock, knock.
Who's there?
Waiter.
Waiter who?
Waiter I get my hands on you.

Knock, knock.
Who's there?
Yoga.
Yoga who?
Yoga what it takes.

Knock, knock.
Who's there?
Orange juice.
Orange juice who?
Orange juice sorry you asked?

Knock, knock.
Who's there?
Boxer.
Boxer who?
Boxer tricks.

Knock, knock.
Who's there?
Almond.
Almond who?
Almond your side, honey!

Knock, knock.
Who's there?
Trixie.
Trixie who?
Trixie couldn't do because he was a bad magician.

Knock, knock.
Who's there?
Ridya.
Ridya who?
Ridya bike and you'll get there quicker.

Knock, knock.
Who's there?
Murray Lee.
Murray Lee who?
Murray Lee rolling along.

Knock, knock.
Who's there?
Spider.
Spider who?
I. Spider with my little eye!

Knock, knock.
Who's there?
Rupert.
Rupert who?
Rupert your left arm in, your left arm out . . .

Knock, knock.
Who's there?
Bingo.
Bingo who?
Bingo'ng to come and see you for ages.